A GUIDE TO

SELECTED POEMS
OF SEAMUS HEANEY

SHAUN McCARTHY

WITH TONY BUZAN

Hodder & Stoughton

Cover photograph ©: Rex Features
Mind Maps: Ann Jones
Illustrations: Karen Donnelly

ISBN 0 340 74766 8

First published 1999
Impression number   10 9 8 7 6 5 4 3 2
Year   2002 2001

Typeset by Transet Limited, Coventry, England.
Printed in Great Britain for Hodder & Stoughton Educational, a division of
Hodder Headline Plc, 338 Euston Road, London NW1 3BH by Cox and Wyman Ltd,
Reading, Berks.

CONTENTS

There are five important things you must know about your brain and memory to revolutionize the way you study:

- ◆ how your memory ('recall') works *while* you are learning
- ◆ how your memory works *after* you have finished learning
- ◆ how to use Mind Maps – a special technique for helping you with all aspects of your studies
- ◆ how to increase your reading speed
- ◆ how to prepare for tests and exams.

Recall during learning
– THE NEED FOR BREAKS

Take reg. breaks - After 20-45 mins can Study

When you are studying, your memory can concentrate, understand and remember well for between 20 and 45 minutes at a time. Then it needs a break. If you carry on for longer than this without a break your memory starts to break down. If you study for hours non-stop, you will remember only a small fraction of what you have been trying to learn, and you will have wasted hours of valuable time.

So, ideally, *study for less than an hour*, then take a five to ten minute break. During the break listen to music, go for a walk, do some exercise, or just daydream. (Daydreaming is a necessary brain-power booster – geniuses do it regularly.) During the break your brain will be sorting out what it has been learning, and you will go back to your books with the new information safely stored and organized in your memory banks. We recommend breaks at regular intervals as you work through the Literature Guides. Make sure you take them!

Recall after learning
– THE WAVES OF YOUR MEMORY

What do you think begins to happen to your memory straight after you have finished learning something? Does it immediately start forgetting? No! Your brain actually *increases* its power and carries on remembering. For a short time after your study session, your brain integrates the information, making a more complete picture of everything it has just learnt. Only then does the rapid decline in memory begin, and as much as 80 per cent of what you have learnt can be forgotten in a day.

However, if you catch the top of the wave of your memory, and briefly review (look back over) what you have been studying at the correct time, the memory is stamped in far more strongly, and stays at the crest of the wave for a much longer time. To maximize your brain's power to remember, take a few minutes and use a Mind Map to review what you have learnt at the end of a day. Then review it at the end of a week, again at the end of a month, and finally a week before your test or exam. That way you'll ride your memory wave all the way there – and beyond!

The Mind Map ®
– A PICTURE OF THE WAY YOU THINK

Do you like taking notes? More importantly, do you like having to go back over and learn them before tests or exams? Most students I know certainly do not! And how do you take your notes? Most people take notes on lined paper, using blue or black ink. The result, visually, is boring! And what does *your* brain do when it is bored? It turns off, tunes out, and goes to sleep! Add a dash of colour, rhythm, imagination, and the whole note-taking process becomes much more fun, uses more of your brain's abilities, and improves your recall and understanding.

A Mind Map mirrors the way your brain works. It can be used for note-taking from books or in class, for reviewing what you have just studied, and for essay planning for coursework and in tests or exams. It uses all your memory's natural techniques to build up your rapidly growing 'memory muscle'.

You will find Mind Maps throughout this book. Study them, add some colour, personalize them, and then have a go at drawing your own – you'll remember them far better! Stick them in your files and on your walls for a quick-and-easy review of the topic.

HOW TO DRAW A MIND MAP

1 Start in the middle of the page. This gives your brain the maximum room for its thoughts.
2 Always start by drawing a small picture or symbol. Why? Because a picture is worth a thousand words to your brain. And try to use at least three colours, as colour helps your memory even more.
3 Let your thoughts flow, and write or draw your ideas on coloured branching lines connected to your central image. These key symbols and words are the headings for your topic. Start like the Mind Map on page 10.
4 Then add facts and ideas by drawing more, smaller, branches on to the appropriate main branches, just like a tree.
5 Always print your word clearly on its line. Use only one word per line.
6 To link ideas and thoughts on different branches, use arrows, colours, underlining, and boxes (see page 25).

HOW TO READ A MIND MAP

1 Begin in the centre, the focus of your topic.
2 The words/images attached to the centre are like chapter headings; read them next.
3 Always read out from the centre, in every direction (even on the left-hand side, where you will have to read from right to left, instead of the usual left to right).

USING MIND MAPS

Mind Maps are a versatile tool – use them for taking notes in class or from books, for solving problems, for brainstorming with friends, and for reviewing and working for tests or exams – their uses are endless! You will find them invaluable for planning essays for coursework and exams. Number your main branches in the order in which you want to use them and off you go – the main headings for your essay are done and all your ideas are logically organized!

Super speed reading

It seems incredible, but it's been proved – the faster you read, the more you understand and remember! So here are some tips to help you to practise reading faster – you'll cover the ground more quickly, remember more, and have more time left for both work and play.

◆ First read the whole text (whether it's a lengthy book or an exam or test paper) very quickly, to give your brain an overall idea of what's ahead and get it working. (It's like sending out a scout to look at the territory you have to cover – it's much easier when you know what to expect!) Then read the text again for more detailed information.
◆ Have the text a reasonable distance away from your eyes. In this way your eye/brain system will be able to see more at a glance, and will naturally begin to read faster.
◆ Take in groups of words at a time. Rather than reading 'slowly and carefully' read faster, more enthusiastically.
◆ Take in phrases rather than single words while you read.
◆ Use a guide. Your eyes are designed to follow movement, so a thin pencil underneath the lines you are reading, moved smoothly along, will 'pull' your eyes to faster speeds.

Preparing for tests and exams

◆ Review your work systematically. Cram at the start of your course, not the end, and avoid 'exam panic'!
◆ Use Mind Maps throughout your course, and build a Master Mind Map for each subject – a giant Mind Map that summarizes everything you know about the subject.
◆ Use memory techniques such as mnemonics (verses or systems for remembering things like dates and events).
◆ Get together with one or two friends to study, compare Mind Maps, and discuss topics.

AND FINALLY...

Have *fun* while you learn – it has been shown that students who make their studies enjoyable understand and remember everything better and get the highest grades. I wish you and your brain every success! (Tony Buzan)

HOW TO USE THIS GUIDE

This guide assumes that you have already read at least some poems by Seamus Heaney, although you could read 'Background' and 'Studying the poems' before that. It is best to use the guide alongside the poems. You could read the 'Themes' section without referring to the poems, but you will get more out of it if you do refer to them to check points made in the section, and especially when thinking about the questions designed to test your recall and help you to think about the poems.

The 'Commentary' section can be used in a number of ways. One way is to read a poem and then read the commentary for that poem, referring to that poem. Another is to read the group of poems from a particular section, and keep on until you come to a test section, test yourself – then have a break! Find out what works best for you.

'Topics for discussion and brainstorming' gives topics that could well feature in exams or provide the basis for coursework. It would be particularly useful for you to discuss them with friends, or brainstorm them using Mind Map techniques (see p. vii).

'How to get an "A" in English Literature' gives valuable advice on what to look for in a text, and what skills you need to develop in order to achieve your personal best.

'The exam essay' is a useful 'night before' reminder of how to tackle exam questions, and 'Model answer' gives an example of an A-grade essay and the Mind Map and plan used to write it.

The questions

Whenever you come across a question in the guide with a star ✪ in front of it, think about it for a moment. You could even jot down a few words in rough to focus your mind. There is not usually a 'right' answer to these questions: it is important for you to develop your own opinions if you want to get an 'A' in your exam. The 'Boost your learning' sections are designed to take you about 10–20 minutes each – which will be time well spent. Take a short break after each one.

 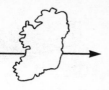

KEY TO ICONS

Themes

A **theme** is an idea explored by the poet. In every commentary there is a section dealing with the theme or themes that the poem explores. This section is introduced by one or more icons indicating what theme(s) the poet is exploring. The icons will help you to see how the themes shown below occur in more than one poem.

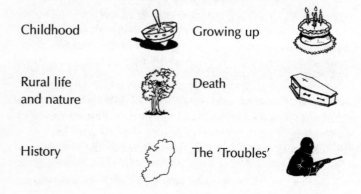

Childhood

Growing up

Rural life
and nature

Death

History

The 'Troubles'

In one or two later poems there is no icon to introduce the themes section because the poem is dealing with a theme not explored by any other poems discussed in the commentaries.

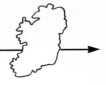

Seamus Heaney – life and works

Seamus Heaney was born at Mossbawn, County Derry, Northern Ireland, in 1939. He was the eldest of nine children. His family were farmers and it was expected that he would continue in this tradition.

He won a scholarship to be a boarding pupil at St Columb's College in the nearby city of Derry when he was 12. He then went on to Queen's University in Belfast, where he studied English. His first poems appeared in the university magazine. Although he admired the skill and dedication of his father he had by now no intention of taking on the farm himself.

Heaney became an English teacher in Belfast. His poems began appearing in small poetry magazines. His first book of poetry, *Death of a Naturalist*, was published in 1966. By now he was a lecturer at Queen's University's English department. *Death of a Naturalist* features a number of poems dealing with his childhood and the loss of innocence that inevitably comes with growing up. It was praised for many qualities including its vivid portrayal of the landscape and way of life of rural Ireland.

Door into the Dark, his second book of poems, was published in 1969. It was a much more confident, risk-taking book. The poems were less personal in their focus. It featured poems about Irish history and culture.

In 1970 he spent a year teaching at Berkeley University in California. He came under the influence of 'free verse' American poets while he was there and his third book, *Wintering Out* (1972), sees him experimenting with a looser style of poetry.

In 1973 Heaney decided to give up lecturing and become a full-time writer. Now a married man with two children, he left Belfast and the 'Troubles' (see A Quick lesson in Irish History overleaf) and moved to a cottage in rural County Wicklow in the Republic of Ireland. By now he enjoyed a reputation as a major poet. He wrote his fourth collection, *North*, while living in

Wicklow. It is the book in which he most directly deals with his thoughts and feelings about the political 'Troubles' in the North he has left behind. He felt very much under pressure at the time to be seen as a poet dealing with the politics and violence of the troubles, but in poems such as 'Punishment' he manages to address these difficult themes in a way that is at once imaginative and intensely human. 'Punishment' also features another key subject that recurs in various poems in *North*: the blackened, eerily-preserved corpses of Iron Age people unearthed in bogs in Ireland and Denmark. The bog landscape had been the background to his own growing up, and when the poet first saw the photographs of these long-dead 'bog people' a connection was made in his creative imagination.

In 1976 the Heaneys moved to Dublin where he became Head of Caryfort Teacher Training College. In 1982 he was appointed Poet in Residence at Harvard University in Boston, and in 1989 became Professor of Poetry at Oxford University. While he occupied these increasingly powerful and prominent positions he published four more collections of poetry: *Station Island* (1984), *The Haw Lantern* (1987), *Seeing Things* (1991) and *The Spirit Level* (1996). He became close friends with other major poets including Ted Hughes, the Poet Laureate who died in 1998, and the Nobel prize-winner Derek Walcott.

In 1995 he was awarded the Nobel Prize for Literature, the highest award a writer can achieve. Not for nothing is he known as 'famous Seamus' to his friends!

A *quick lesson in Irish history*

The following poems discussed in the commentaries feature themes about Irish politics and history: 'Requiem for the Croppies', 'Dedicatory Poem from *Wintering Out*', ' Funeral Rites', 'Punishment', 'Act of Union', 'Singing School 2: A Constable Calls', and 'Casualty'.

The following background historical information will help you to understand these poems. It will also give you a useful insight into the background of the society in which Heaney grew up and has lived for most of his life. Although most of us have seen news reports of the 'Troubles' in Northern Ireland, Irish history is rarely taught in British schools.

HISTORY AND HEANEY

Heaney grew up in a society divided by religion, Catholic and Protestant. The Heaney family were Catholic. The ruling group in Northern Ireland were Protestant and there was widespread discrimination against Catholics. The seeds of what would flare into the violence, bombing and rioting that lasted on and off from 1969 to 1998 in Northern Ireland were present in Heaney's everyday life as a young boy.

Heaney's first collection of poems, *Death of a Naturalist*, focused almost entirely on personal subjects, but there is a sort of 'middle period' where he deals much more directly with the 'Troubles' and their historical roots. When he was writing these poems Heaney was becoming recognized as perhaps the most successful and important poet to come out of Northern Ireland this century and he has said that he felt a duty and a responsibility to write about what was happening there.

Further reading You might enjoy comparing Heaney's political poems with those written by the great Irish poet W.B. Yeats, who wrote about violent political events in the Easter 1916 Uprising in Dublin. Try comparing his poems 'Easter 1916' and 'Sixteen Dead Men' with Heaney's 'Casualty'.

ULSTER AND EIRE

Northern Ireland is also known as Ulster. It consists of the six northern counties of the island of Ireland and is joined politically to Great Britain and the British Government in Westminster. The rest of Ireland, the 'south' or Eire, is an independent republic. Although British citizens are exempt from the need to take their passports when they travel there, it is in all other ways as separate from Great Britain as Spain or China.

How did this strange partition of Ireland into two completely separate parts come about? Read on to find out.

THE NORMAN INVASION OF IRELAND

The history of the conflict in Northern Ireland can be traced right back to the twelfth century. Rivalry and skirmishing between Irish tribes allowed well-organized Norman war parties to sail over from Britain to conquer and settle parts of eastern Ireland, around what is now Dublin. The area they colonised became known as 'the Pale'. People living within the Pale owed allegiance to the King of England.

IRELAND AND THE TUDORS

In the sixteenth century England had become a Protestant country but the majority of Irish were devoutly Catholic. They wanted independence from England. The English feared that Catholic Spain would send troops and weapons to the Irish to help them reclaim their independence. The English settlers extended their colonies and power throughout Ireland in order to stop this happening. The powerful Earls of Ulster led a rebellion against the English, but the military help they were waiting for from Spain didn't arrive. The uprising failed and in 1602 the earls fled to the continent.

THE ROOTS OF ENGLISH CLAIMS ON NORTHERN IRELAND (ULSTER)

James I of England seized the lands of the earls who had led the unsuccessful rebellion. These were all in the North. He knew that it was this part of Ireland that most threatened his power. He colonized the lands he had seized with loyal subjects from England and Scotland. Only a small area within each of the counties in this area was reserved for the native Irish who had lived there all along. The new settlers built fortified enclosures. They brought their own Protestant religion with them. This was the beginning of the religious divisions that still trouble Northern Ireland today.

THE 1641 REBELLION

England remained worried by the possibility of a rebellion by Catholics in Ireland. Most of the powerful nations of Europe were Catholic. Spain in particular was thought to be prepared to help Ireland fight for its independence. The English were forced to maintain a standing army of occupation in Ireland. Northern Ireland, or Ulster, was still seen as the most likely place for trouble to begin, and in 1641 there was a rebellion. The fighting went on sporadically for ten years until the arrival of Oliver Cromwell.

OLIVER CROMWELL

The English king Charles I had been forced from power and executed by Cromwell. Cromwell was a ruthless military leader and a zealous puritan who hated Catholicism. He decided to crush the power of the rebel Irish and landed his 'New Model Army' in Ireland in 1649. Three thousand Irish were killed in the first battle and Cromwell began a nine-month campaign of utter savagery against both Irish troops and civilians. He awarded lands he had captured throughout Ireland to those who had supported him.

JAMES II

This English king (1685–8) was much more tolerant towards the Catholics in Ireland. He appointed the Irish Catholic Earl Tyrconnel to the post Lord Lieutenant, the representative of the British crown in Ireland. Tyrconnel dismissed all Protestants from the army of occupation and weakened this force by sending troops to England to support the king there. The Protestants in Ulster were worried by all this. When William of Orange, a Protestant, was declared king of England by his supporters over James, the Ulster Protestants saw a powerful new figurehead for their cause.

The two kings, James and William were vying for the English throne. The outcome was decided in Ireland in 1690 at the Battle of the Boyne. James was defeated, England got a new king, and the power of the Protestants in Ulster was made secure. After the defeat of the Catholic army at the Boyne discrimination against Irish Catholics, the vast majority of the population, got underway. Catholics were denied the vote and even the right to own land. They had to pay high rents to farm land that had been given to Protestants.

CONTINUING UNREST

Throughout the 1700s there was unrest and violence throughout Ireland as Catholics sort to improve the terrible conditions they were forced to endure. The suffering of the Catholics fuelled a small and unsuccessful uprising in Armagh after which Protestants formed The Orange Society (in honour of William of Orange) which aimed to ensure that Protestants always maintained power over Catholics. This became known as the 'Protestant Ascendancy'. 'Loyal Orange Lodges' still exist throughout Northern Ireland and they still march every summer to celebrate the victory of William over James.

BATTLE OF VINEGAR HILL

Sporadic rebel action expanded into full scale rebellion in 1798. After a nine-month campaign 20,000 poorly-armed rebels were surrounded and massacred at Vinegar Hill in the south west of Ireland. The victorious Protestants convinced the British government at Westminster that effective law had broken down in Ireland and the Act of Union was passed in 1800 abolishing the Irish government and linking Ireland to Britain 'for ever'. Many of the big landlords who had opposed this bill left their lands in the hands of agents and moved to England. This 'absentee landlord' system was to cause trouble in the future, because tenants were paying high rents while enduring terrible living conditions.

At the same time Ulster was developing a separate economy and identity from the rest of Ireland. It had a very successful linen weaving industry employing thousands of home-based workers. The rest of Ireland survived on small scale farming.

THE FAMINE

In 1845 Ireland was one of the most densely populated countries in Europe (contrast this with Irish Tourist Board advertisements for their country today as a quiet and empty 'get away from the crowds' destination – which it is).

Most of the population were desperately poor and depended on potatoes for their main source of food. The crop failed in 1845 and again in the following two years. A million people starved to death. The British government provided almost no help. Another million Irish were forced to emigrate, mostly to America. They endured terrible crossings on crowded 'coffin ships'. Many emigrants, already weak from starvation, died on the crossing. In a few years the population of Ireland had been reduced by half.

ULSTER AND HOME RULE

Unlike most of Ireland, where small-scale farming was the main occupation, engineering developed in Ulster, especially

7

ship-building in Belfast. In the 1860s the city was one of the main industrial centres in Great Britain.

The English Prime Minister William Gladstone believed that some form of home rule was necessary to solve the problems of trying to govern Ireland. Protestants, especially those in Ulster, opposed any form of home rule. The battle lines began to be drawn that led right up to the 'Troubles' of the 1960s–90s. Protestants fearing an end to the Protestant Ascendancy formed a rebel group, the Ulster Volunteers, dedicated to protecting their interests. The Catholics who wanted home rule formed the Irish Volunteers.

At the beginning of this century there were many moves to 're-discover' Irish culture and traditions. Celtic myths and legends became part of the work of writers such as the poet W.B. Yeats and the playwright J.M. Synge. This recognition of Irish culture gradually spread from artists through society, and many people began to see just how different they, as Irish men and women, were to the British that had so long colonized and controlled their land.

THE *1916* UPRISING

An extremist Nationalist group, the Irish Republican Brotherhood, took advantage of British involvement in the First World War to launch an uprising in Dublin during Easter week, 1916. After several days of heavy fighting, in which British artillery was used to bombard buildings in the capital city, the rebels surrendered. They had not enjoyed much public support. But this changed when the British government began executing rebel leaders. The rebels began to be seen as martyrs by more and more of the people of Ireland.

WAR AND INDEPENDENCE

Civil war against British rule broke out in 1920. One of Ireland's most charismatic leaders, Michael Collins, led the nationalist forces of rebellion (nationalist = one who wants to create an independent Irish nation). The British government could not protect Protestant Unionists (Unionist = one who wants to stay within the union of Great Britain) living in the predominantly Catholic south nor Catholics living in the predominantly Unionist Ulster.

The British government partitioned Ireland into two separate areas: Southern Ireland and Ulster or Northern Ireland. It was designed to be a temporary arrangement to help Britain maintain control over the country. The south became known as the Irish Free State. It was to be a dominion (like many semi-independent countries in the old British Commonwealth) and was not as tightly bound to Britain as the North.

A border was drawn between the North and the Free State. Towns were divided in such a way as to ensure a Unionist Protestant majority in every border area in the North. Throughout the North voting constituencies were drawn up to ensure that Catholic residents were never in a majority and could therefore never elect a representative to government. Denying Catholics a say in running the North in this way was one of the main causes of the 'Troubles'.

In 1932 the Free State of Ireland declared itself an independent republic.

CIVIL RIGHTS AND THE 'TROUBLES'

Discrimination against Catholics in the North meant their living conditions and opportunities were far worse than for most other people in Great Britain. They were denied access to better housing and many types of jobs were effectively reserved for Protestants. Frustration with a voting system that denied Catholics a political voice led to the formation of the Northern Civil Rights Association in 1967.

In 1968, during a peaceful rally, Civil Rights marchers were attacked by baton-wielding members of the RUC (Royal Ulster Constabulary), a police force almost entirely made up of Protestant officers. This was the spark that led to the explosion of the 'Troubles' in 1969.

Soon after this the British army were drafted into Northern Ireland to try to keep the peace between Protestant Unionists and Catholic Nationalists. Both sides developed terrorist groups who murdered and bombed. Towns in Northern Ireland were divided into Protestant and Catholic areas, sometimes with security walls constructed between them. Fortified police and army posts were built. Some areas became so dangerous for the security forces that they could only supply their forts by helicopter. Thousands of people on both sides of the conflict have been killed, including many innocent victims of the huge bombs that were regularly set off by either side to create terror and to try to make Northern Ireland ungovernable.

In 1997 a ceasefire was agreed by both sides, but it broke down. At the time of writing, 1998, a new ceasefire seems to be holding despite a terrible bomb blast in Omagh that killed over 20 shoppers one Saturday afternoon. The horror of this event seems to have persuaded both Protestant and Catholic terrorist groups to lay down their guns and their bombs.

Boost your learning

This Mini Mind Map will help you sort out the political divisions in Northern Ireland, which is important background for Heaney's political poems. Copy it out onto a big sheet of paper and add your ideas to it when you read these poems: 'Dedicatory poem from *Wintering Out*', 'Funeral Rites', 'Punishment' and 'Casualty'.

Reading the poems

Before you begin studying the poems of Seamus Heaney in depth, making notes etc, read them at least once just for pleasure. Ask yourself how you feel about a poem, what response it sparks in you and what you like about it.

Take a few moments break after each poem to 'let it sink in'. Don't expect the poems to reveal all their levels of meaning to you in one easy go. Most of these poems are the result of many hours hard work and craftsmanship, and they contain lots of information and ideas.

Reading them aloud lets you hear the rhythm of the language and the rhymes (if there are any). Many poets believe poems only really 'come alive' when read aloud. Although you will be concerned with finding out the exact meaning of the poems and of lines within the poems, never lose sight of the fact that poems are written to create not just an intellectual response, but an emotional one as well. It's all right to say, to begin with anyway, 'I don't really know what it means, but I like the sound and the feel of the words.'   ＼ok to not understand at first

Asking questions

Now you can start to work out what the poem is about and how it works. Begin by asking yourself a few basic questions about each poem.

Who is 'speaking' the poem? Is it the poet, the poet as a younger version of himself (which is the case with a lot of Heaney's earlier poems), or a character?

What is the emotional tone of the poem? Does the poet 'sound' angry, happy, sad, wistful, coolly analytic etc? Much of Heaney's work is quiet and balanced, he relies on his intelligence and skill at telling a story or creating a picture to carry the emotional impact of the poem, rather than being

even though he speaks from the heart

more obviously emotional. Although he speaks from the heart, he does not 'rant and rave'.

Is the poem dealing with a subject or a theme that has occurred in another poem you have read by Heaney? Most writers, including Heaney, return to ideas that interest them and work with them in different ways.

How is the poem laid out on the page?

◆ Is the poem written in verses? If so, does each verse have the same number of lines?

◆ Are the lines long or short, or a mixture of lengths? Is there a pattern to this?

◆ Do most lines end with commas or full stops or does the meaning run over into the next line? If it does, can you say why the poet stops the lines where he does?

◆ Does the structure of the poem link up with what it is about? For instance does it imitate the way a person might speak? Does the structure create a special effect? How?

◆ Are there rhymes at the end of lines? Is there a pattern to the rhymes? Do the lines have a set rhythm of beats or stresses? Can you find out what this set rhythm is?

To help you answer questions about rhyme and rhythm, look at the 'Poetic Form and Structure' notes on p. 14.

Identify lines that contain phrases or images that puzzle you. Do the same for vocabulary. Find out the meaning of any words that you don't know. There may be words which you do know but which the poet is using in a way that may be confusing. Poets sometimes play with double meanings. See if this is being done in the poem you are reading. Most poems are quite 'intense', they say a lot more in a few lines than most prose does. You have to read a poem very carefully several times to see all the levels of meaning it may have.

Check any references to things and events that you don't understand. The 'Style and references' sections of the commentaries in these notes will list all the references that may cause problems.

*S*ubject and theme

Now you need to think in depth and detail about what the poet is saying. This can sometimes seem a bit like cracking a code. But most of Heaney's poetry is quite straightforward and with these notes to help you, it should not present any serious difficulties.

The most important thing to do when studying a poem is to try to separate the two levels of meaning that almost all poems have in some form or another: the **subject** and **theme**. These are key concepts and understanding how they operate will make your revision of the poems in this selection both easier and more thorough.

The **subject** is what the poem is about: the event, scene or person it describes, the story it tells etc. So a poem about a cat owned by an old lady entitled 'The Wonderful Tiddles' may describe, from the old lady's point of view, the appearance of her beloved cat, the wonderful things it does etc. The cat is the subject of the poem.

What it describes

The **theme** is the idea, emotion, philosophy etc, that underlies the subject. The theme gives the poem its intellectual and emotional depth. So our imaginary poem 'The Wonderful Tiddles' could have as its theme the loneliness of old age when the only companion an old lady has is a cat that basically just eats and sleeps. Or it could be that the cat really is a wonderful and unique creature, and the theme now would be the wisdom of age which allows the old lady to understand the cat's secret qualities.

What idea it deals with!
- loneliness
- Troubles
- Irish history
- childhood
- Agriculture

A more complex example of the subject – theme way of constructing a poem would be Heaney's 'The Forge'. On a first reading, this poem is simply a piece of descriptive writing. It paints a vivid and detailed picture of a blacksmith who keeps his forge going despite the fact that there are fewer and fewer horses and more and more motor cars. The world does not need his skills in the way it once did, but he carries on because he is a craftsman who believes in the quality and value of his skilled work. This is the subject of the poem.

But careful reading of the poem (and of the commentary on it in these notes!) will reveal that it has a completely different theme underlying this subject. Heaney is actually using the blacksmith and his commitment to his art as a symbol for the way creative artists, including poets, stick to what they are doing because they have the skills and believe their art is important. This is the theme of the poem.

Subjects are 'concrete', they are stories, scenes, events from the real world. You can almost see and touch the subject of really good poems. Themes are 'abstract', they are ideas, beliefs, philosophies, emotions. They exist in the heart and the mind.

Most 'serious' poets like Heaney use a subject to convey a theme. This double layer of content and meaning gives poems depth. It makes them more interesting and worth re-reading. It also means that the entire meaning does not always spring out from the page after just one reading.

Understanding this division between subject and theme is vital if you want to understand Heaney's poems fully. In the commentaries the introductory section tells you what the subject is, and the 'Themes' section explains the themes underlying the subject.

Poems can have more than one theme. Refer to the icons at the beginning of the 'Themes' sections to see which theme(s) each poem is dealing with. The icons also show you how certain themes recur in different ways in Heaney's poems.

Sometimes the subject and theme of a poem are so closely linked that it is not profitable to try to separate them. This rarely happens with Heaney, but in the one or two examples where this is the case the commentary explains how the poem operates.

Poetic form and structure

This section gives you a few tips on working out how a poem is structured, why it looks as it does on the page and why it sounds as it does when read aloud.

Poetry is distinct from prose in one fundamental way: it has some sort of rhythm and possibly rhyme built into it. This makes a poem more like song lyrics than like a paragraph from a novel. This structure might not always be easy to see or hear, but you should try to at least mention the basic structure of a poem when writing about it.

Some poets write very traditionally. They set up a strict pattern of line lengths, of beats in each line and rhymes and then 'pour' their poetic ideas into this mould. This was how almost all poetry was written up to the beginning of this century. Then there appeared various writers who tried to get away from writing in these strict traditional forms. Their ideas were very influential and today there are a lot of poets who write 'free verse' where there is no continuous strict pattern of lines, rhymes or rhythms through the poem, but a looser more flowing structure based on the way words in each line work together.

The poems of Seamus Heaney covered in this guide tend to be basically traditional in structure, but with an easy fluidity and confidence to stretch or bend the patterns when the poet thinks the meaning needs it. His way of working could be likened to a musician who sets up a basic rhythm, then moves in and out of it to suit what he is playing.

The two basic elements of the structure of a poem are line length and beats, and rhyme.

LINE LENGTH AND RHYTHM

When we speak we stress certain words in a phrase or syllables within words. This doesn't vary: we always put the emphasis on the second syllable of 'destroy' but on the first syllable of 'certain' (try doing it the other way round and see how odd it sounds). But in normal conversation we don't usually hear the difference between stressed (emphasized) and unstressed (un-emphasized) syllables.

But poets use this natural stressed and unstressed, or hard and soft, system of syllables to construct patterns and create rhythms in their lines. There is a whole complex study of this called 'prosody' which you do not need to bother about, but you do need to know a few basic rules to help you appreciate the technical qualities of Seamus Heaney's poetry.

Lines of poetry are generally measured by the number of stressed syllables, also called beats, they contain (usually two, three, four or five stressed syllables or beats). Unstressed syllables are less important. Working out the pattern of stressed and unstressed syllables in a line is called 'scanning' and is usually done by putting a slash symbol (/) above every stressed syllable and a dash symbol (–) above the unstressed ones. And the usual pattern is either alternating unstressed/stressed syllables, – / , or sometimes unstressed/unstressed/stressed – – /. These little groups of two or three syllables are called 'feet' and the number of feet you have determines the number of beats and the line length.

Look at this line from 'Digging'. Say it out loud and see how the scanning shows where the stresses or beats (/) fall.

```
 – /      – / – / – /
Between my finger and my thumb
```

You certainly do not have to go through scanning every line in every Seamus Heaney poem you study, but it can be helpful to try to do it for a few lines to get an idea of the pattern of beats per line he is setting up in a poem. At least you can then say in an answer that the basic line length in a poem is three, four or however many beats per line.

Heaney is not generally a strict keeper of rhythm in every line. Most of his poems have a basic pattern or number of beats per line but he carefully varies this to suit the sense and mood of what he is saying.

Find the pattern

Use the – and / symbols to scan these lines from 'Requiem for the Croppies'. Can you find the common pattern of each line? To help you do this read them aloud slowly.

No kitchens on the run, no striking camp –
A people hardly marching – on the hike –
We'd cut through reins and rider with the pike

(Check your work with the answer on p. 19 at the end of this section.)

RHYME

The 'Structure' section of the commentaries on each poem discussed in this guide tells you if there is a rhyme scheme or pattern. It describes this in terms of, for example ABAB...

But what does this mean?

To find out if a poem has a rhyme scheme, start by reading it aloud. In the selection of poems dealt with in this guide you need only worry about finding patterns of rhyming words at the ends of lines.

If you think there is a rhyme pattern or scheme, put an A at the end of the first line and look down to see which line or lines rhyme with it. Mark them with an A as well. Then see if the end word of the second line rhymes with any other lines. If it does mark these with Bs and so on. Not all lines in the rhymed poem necessarily rhyme; there may be some you just have to leave blank. When you have found all the rhymes, look at the pattern of As, Bs, Cs, etc, you have made.

To go back to the example at the beginning of this section, if the first and third and second and fourth lines in a poem are rhyming pairs then this will be shown as ABAB.

Find the rhymes

Read the first verse of 'Personal Helicon' below and mark the rhyme scheme at the end of these lines. (Reading it aloud will help.)

> *As a child, they could not keep me from wells*
> *And old pumps with buckets and windlasses.*
> *I loved the dark drop, the trapped sky, the smells*
> *Of waterweed, fungus and dank moss.*

If you have a bit of struggle with this, it is because Heaney uses half rhymes a lot to soften the 'chiming' effect of too many pure rhymes. One of the pairs of rhymes you should have found in this extract is a full or pure rhyme, the other is only a half rhyme.

Now look up the poem and mark the rhyme scheme for the other four verses.

INTERNAL RHYMES

Sometimes poems have 'internal rhymes', where any word in a line rhymes with a word in the same postion in another line. In Heaney's poems this type of rhyme is not nearly as common as end rhyme but it does occur. ✪ Can you find an internal rhyme in the lines given as an answer on p. 19?

ALLITERATION AND ASSONANCE

Look out for alliteration and assonance in the poems. Alliteration is where two or more words close together (in the same line) sound very similar. For example: *shilly-shallied/scaresomely* ('Seeing Things'). Assonance is the rhyming of two words on their vowels but not their consonants, creating a sort of half rhyme or echo. For example, one/reflection ('Personal Helicon'), where the 'o' links the sound of the two words.

IMAGERY

Heaney uses language simply but to great effect. He is skilled at 'painting pictures in words'. Imagery is a vital part of this. An **image** is a way of describing something in a new, fresh and imaginatibe way, usually in a few words or a short phrase.

In the second verse of 'Death of a Naturalist' Heaney describes frogs sitting *poised like mud grenades*. Grenades are grey-green and sit motionless until they suddenly explode – rather like these frogs. The child is the poem is afraid of the frogs because they might suddenly jump or make a noise and scare him. They have the same general air of waiting, suspended menace as a live grenade. This is an example of Heaney using language simply but with great accuracy and imagination. This particular image is a **simile**: it describes the frogs as being *similar* to grenades.

Another kind of image with Heaney uses is the **metaphor**. A metaphor described something as though it were something else. For example: *the chin is a visor* ('The Grauballe Man'). A metaphor is like a compressed simile.

You can find images that use language like this in most of Heaney's poems. Some imagery pushes language to the limits of its meaning and sometimes you need to read the line or phrase very carefully to see exactly what the poet means.

ANSWER TO 'FIND THE PATTERN' (P.16)

```
 –   /   –   /  –  /  –  /  –    /
No kitchens on the run, no striking camp –
 –  /  –  /  –  /   –    /  –  /
A people hardly marching – on the hike –
 –   /   –    /  –  /–  /  –  /
We'd cut through reins and rider with the pike
```

The internal rhyme is between *run*, in line 1, and *reins*, in line 3.

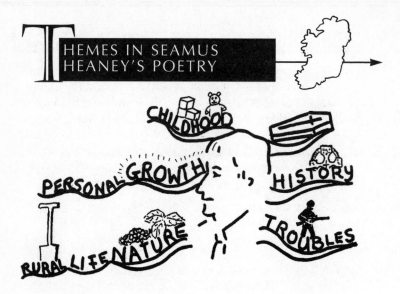

THEMES IN SEAMUS HEANEY'S POETRY

A **theme** is an idea developed or explored throughout a work. The main themes of Heaney's poetry are shown in the Mini Mind Map above. Test yourself by copying it, adding to it when you read the commentaries, then comparing your results with the version on p. 25. (Don't worry if they're not exactly the same, but you should see the overall pattern of connections.)

The poems in the Commentaries section of this guide have been chosen to show both the range and variety of ideas in Heaney's writing and his returning to certain key themes which have inspired more than one poem. Often these recurring themes have appeared in poems written many years apart.

When planning an exam answer it can be very helpful to show that you understand how two or more poems connect through a shared theme. Seeing how the poet approaches an idea in different ways in different poems allows you to speak more about the way he works generally and not just to make comments on individual poems.

The 'themes' section of the commentaries begin with one or more icons identifying the theme(s) of the poem. You have already met these in the 'Key to Icons' section of this guide (p. x).

Childhood

Many of the earliest poems discussed in this guide, those that appeared in Heaney's first book *Death of a Naturalist*, feature this theme. It is often dealt with in connection with the idea of growing up and leaving childhood innocence behind (see next theme below). Heaney is perhaps best known for the scenes of rural childhood that he described in poems such as 'Death of a Naturalist', 'Cow in Calf', 'Blackberry-Picking' and 'Personal Helicon'.

Childhood is also a theme to which he has returned, sometimes as a father observing his own or other peoples' children, and sometimes as an older man remembering his own childhood, in some of his later poems. Curiously, 'Wheels Within Wheels', a later poem where he recalls scenes from his now long-ago childhood, has almost exactly the same tone and atmosphere as the poems about childhood written almost thirty years before it.

Growing up

This was another recurring theme in *Death of a Naturalist*. In vivid, often quite violent images, especially in the book's title poem, Heaney shows how a child's innocent and optimistic view of the world, usually the world of nature, is soon disappointed by reality. Things change, innocence is lost. The frogspawn hatches into frightening and threatening frogs. In 'Blackberry-Picking' the pleasure of collecting tins of rich, ripe berries is destroyed as they start to rot. The world Heaney describes is one in which there is a constant sense of disappointment and even danger lurking in the apparently idyllic countryside. But there is also a feeling that this process, this realizing the world for what it really is, is inevitable. It has happened to everybody. Although for the child in the poems the world has changed, it is the young Heaney growing up who is changing the most.

This sense of growing self-awareness and growing into adulthood reaches a climax in the last poem in *Death of a Naturalist*. 'Personal Helicon' offers the sort of vivid, 'childs-eye' views of the domestic world of the farm where Heaney grew up that occur throughout the book. He describes a free and easy boy exploring different types of wells, but the poem ends with the poet realizing that he has a mission now, to become a writer. The time for games and playful explorations is over.

Rural life and nature

Throughout the poems in the selection, Heaney provides fascinating views and descriptions of rural life, of the farming and country landscape of County Derry. He describes in detail the farming activities of his father (ploughing in 'The Follower') and grandfather (cutting turf from the bog in 'Digging'). The picture Heaney paints of the country life into which he was born is of a world and a society which is changing both through time and the seasons, and enduring and lasting because each generation takes on the way of life of its forebears.

Time also animates the rural images that Heaney uses in other poems where he emphasizes the inevitable cycle of growth and harvest, birth and death. 'At a Potato Digging' describes modern-day farm workers doing more or less exactly the same work as their ancestors who suffered in the Famine. In 'Requiem for the Croppies' the first and most natural requiem or memorial the slaughtered rebels have is the barley they carried in their pockets growing out of their mass, unmarked graves.

Death

A theme which has preoccupied many poets through history, death is dealt with in a unique and fascinating way by Heaney in his poems about 'bog-people'. Three examples are discussed in the Commentaries section of this guide: 'The Tollund Man', 'The Grauballe Man' and 'Punishment'. All these poems consider how and why the person whose preserved body has been dug out of the bog died. 'The Tollund Man' links the long-ago death with the murders of people caught up in the 'Troubles' of Northern Ireland.

Heaney has also written about deaths of a much more personal kind: see 'A Mid-Term Break', 'Funeral Rites' and 'Casualty'.

History

Heaney is deeply concerned with history, especially Irish history. Through history he attempts to find his own identity as an Irishman and a poet living through the 'Troubles' in Northern Ireland.

For Heaney, history is much more than just the study of past events. It is cyclical, it can repeat itself. He sees this happening in Northern Ireland with the 'Troubles' being, on one level, just another manifestation of the violence that has flared up throughout Irish history as a result of colonialism and occupation.

The traces of past events are seen by the poet in the landscape all around him (see the commentary on 'Bogland'). History is a continuing process and the times we live in, and the part the poet plays in our times, are all a part of it.

The 'Troubles'

When the 'Troubles' were at their height, in the very late 1960s and through the 1970s, Heaney's reputation was growing. He was being regarded by more and more people as the major poet in Northern Ireland. He is on record as saying he felt a responsibility to write about the events that were being seen by the world through the news media. He was very aware that Irish history is not widely understood outside of Ireland and he used references to other histories (see the section on the theme of Death, above) to help people understand the causes of the violence that was sweeping Northern Ireland.

But Heaney's responses to the murders and bombings are also intensely personal. 'Casualty' is at once a poem about an event which is small in terms of the suffering of Northern Ireland, the death of one very ordinary, unknown man. But in its depth of passion for this one event, Heaney has focused readers on the real human cost and tragedy of the violence in Northern Ireland more powerfully that almost any other writer.

There are several other themes which occur in only one poem each in the Commentaries. These have not been given icons but are described in the 'Themes' section of the commentary of the poem where they occur.

Boost your learning

?   Now read 'Death of a Naturalist'. Write down a few lines about how you imagine the child to feel at the beginning of the poem and at the end. Then look at 'Blackberry Picking': do you think there are similarities in the feelings the child has here to the feelings expressed in 'Death of a Naturalist'? Describe what you think these feeling are in a few words.

?   Now try a more difficult comparison between poems that share some thematic ideas. Read 'Casualty' and 'The Tollund Man.' Write a few lines explaining the main similarities and differences between the men who died. Think about how they died. Were they both in some ways responsible for their own deaths?

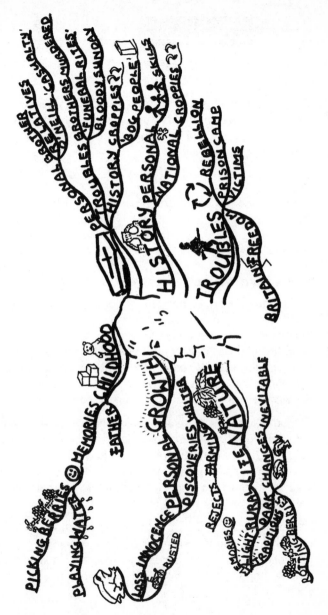

Studying themes is hard work. Take a break.

COMMENTARIES

Each commentary begins with an introductory section, and then focuses in turn on Structure, Themes, Style and references (looking at the use and meanings of the words used), and Links to other poems by Heaney.

ICONS

Wherever there is a focus on a particular theme, the icon for that theme appears in the margin (see p.x for key). See how the theme emerges in the poem. You could also refer back to the 'Themes' chapter.

BOOSTING YOUR LEARNING

At the end of every commentary a 'Boost your learning' section gives one or more activities to reinforce your understanding of the poem. These are to help you revise. You do not have to write detailed and perfect answers to a question. A Mini Mind Map or a few quickly jotted notes will work much better. Sometimes the activity will ask you to link together the knowledge you have of two or more poems.

A good way to use these activities to help you revise is to work with a friend. Brainstorm ideas together. Sharing your ideas will help you see things in the poem you had missed or help you remember things you had forgotten. Working on a Mind Map together also helps you get a clear picture of what the poems are about.

At the end of some 'Boost your learning' sections there are tasks that ask you to look at several poems together. These are designed to help you see Heaney's work as a related body of writing, not just individual poems with no connection to each other.

Digging

Heaney says this was his first 'real' poem. It is about himself, as a young man, making a decision about his future life. The poet is writing in his room, possibly writing this poem. He hears his father digging in the family garden. His father is an expert with a spade, as was his father before him. The poet recalls being a young boy gathering potatoes as his father was digging them up. He then remembers taking milk up to his grandfather who was cutting turf in the bogs. His grandfather was famous locally for the amount of turf he could cut in a day. The poet is aware that good spade work is an important skill linking generations and members of his farming family.

The poem ends with the poet deciding that he does not have the skill for farming work that his father and grandfather had. He considers the pen in his hand, and decides that he will become an expert with that instead.

Structure The poem is written in loose irregular lines, as though someone were thinking aloud. There are a few strong rhymes at the end of lines. ✪ Find these rhymes.

 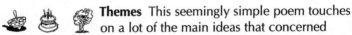 **Themes** This seemingly simple poem touches on a lot of the main ideas that concerned Heaney as a young poet. His connection to his family is very important. His early decision to be a writer not a farmer is one that shaped the rest of his life. As in many of his early poems, 'Digging' describes country skills and scenes very vividly.

There is also a hint of danger. The poet begins by comparing his pen with a gun. Although the 'Troubles' had not yet begun when this poem was written (in 1964) there was a sense that danger was never far away in Northern Ireland. A pen can be used to write things that can inspire people to riot and violence, or to draft an appeal for peace. Heaney is hinting at the power that a writer can have over events.

Style and references The poet uses all the senses in the descriptions of his father and his grandfather digging. The language is simple. Apart from comparing his pen to a gun, there are no similes, metaphors or images, just clear descriptions of men working.

potato drills (line 8) – lines of potato plants.

turf (line 17) – much of Ireland is covered by peat bogs. The peat is cut out in spade-sized sections or 'sods', stacked up and left to dry. It is then called turf and is burnt on fires like logs.

Links 'Death of a Naturalist', 'Cow in Calf', 'At a Potato Digging', 'Personal Helicon' and 'Wheels within Wheels' all contain detailed descriptions from the poet's rural childhood. 'Follower' also has the poet admiring the practical skills of his father.

Boost your learning

?   Find at least one example each of smell, sight, sound and touch in the descriptions of digging.

?   Make a Mini Mind Map of the poet's relationship with the men digging in this poem.

Death of a Naturalist

In the first verse the poet describes how as a child he collected frogspawn from stagnant water. He describes the scene in great detail and creates a sense of summer heat and calm. He takes the frogspawn to school and the teacher explains the process by which the spawn is created. He quotes the words the primary school teacher uses – 'mammy frog' and 'daddy frog' – which heighten our sense of seeing the scene through the eyes of a child. There is an atmosphere of innocent childhood throughout the first verse.

In the second verse the boy returns to the dam but now a sense of danger and menace begins to grow. The frogs' croaking is 'coarse', they 'slap and pop' as they jump into the water and this sounds to him like 'obscene threats'. He feels that if he puts his hand in the water it will somehow be trapped by the floating frogspawn. He is sickened by the scene that he previously enjoyed and he runs away.

Notice that there is no mention of frogs in the first verse, but they dominate the scene described in the second verse.

Structure This poem is divided into two unequal verses of 20 then 12 lines. The lines are of uneven lengths and there are no end rhymes.

Themes The theme of the poem is a journey from innocence to a sense of fear. The trigger for this journey seems to be the teacher's explanation of what frogspawn is. The poem presents the same scene of the flax dam and the frogs in two lights: first, an innocent vision of childhood pleasure, second a place of unpleasant smells, decay, and potential danger. There is no actual danger from the frogs, but the boy's sense of wonder has been replaced by a feeling of brooding horror. The poet is using this event as a powerful example of the way things in our childhood lose their magic as we grow up and learn more about the darker side of the world. ❂ Has anything actually changed at the flax dam between the two visits?

Style and references Heaney uses some very vivid images to convey an innocent, childlike view of the world in the first verse:

bubbles gargled delicately, bluebottles/
wove a strong gauze of sound
But best of all was the warm thick slobber around the smell ...
of frogspawn

Compare these descriptions and images to the language used in the second verse where the sense of menace predominates:

angry frogs/invaded the flax dam
coarse crocking
gross bellied frogs
mud grenades
their blunt heads farting
slime kings

A *flax dam* is a bank beside water where flax that has been cut in the fields is piled up to dry. It is then used to make linen. Linen making was a major industry in Northern Ireland so flax dams would have been a common sight in the poet's childhood.

❂ Find words in the poem where the sound, when said aloud, echoes the actual sounds you might have heard at the dam. (This is called **onomatopoeia**.)

Links The idea of something natural, which is at first attractive, having a dark side which gradually turns pleasure to horror, is also explored in 'Blackberry Picking' and 'Personal Helicon'.

Boost your learning

?   Make a Mini Mind Map of the ideas you have about this poem. Start with two branches, one for the first and one for the second verse.

?   Why is this poem called 'Death of a Naturalist'? Who or what has 'died'?

?   Find references to weapons and war in 'Death of a Naturalist'.

Blackberry-Picking

In the first long verse the poet remembers gathering blackberries as a child. The images are full of pleasure and even sensuality. Only towards the end of this verse is there a hint that something might be wrong.

The second verse takes the action forward a few days. The gathered berries are beginning to stink and rot. The child, the young poet, feels like crying at the unfairness of this. There is sadness is the final lines when the boy says that each year he hopes the sweetness of the fruit will last, even though he knows it must always rot and stink.

Structure   The poem is written in two verses, the first of 16 lines, the second of eight. There are some rhymes and half rhymes, but no regular pattern. ❂ Find the rhymes.

Themes   The whole poem is an **extended metaphor**. It is charged with suppressed emotion, much stronger than one might expect to have for a simple pleasure like blackberrying. While the subject is the simple activity of fruit gathering followed by the rot that sets in to the stored berries, the theme of the poem is the brief and passing nature of pleasure.

The poet's underlying idea is that desiring something, and then obtaining it, all too quickly leads to disappointment and sadness when it ends. The images the poet uses suggest very strongly that sexual passion and its satisfaction are really the main subject of this poem. The poet as a young boy is just awakening to sexual passion.

Style and references There is a dark strand of images running through this poem, even in the first verse which describes a fondly remembered childhood scene. These dark images include:

a glossy purple clot – hinting at blood.
big dark blobs burned/like a plate of eyes
palms sticky as Bluebeard's – Bluebeard was a notoriously bloody pirate figure, who murdered his wife for entering a forbidden room in his castle.

✪ All these quotes are from the first verse. Find examples of dark and unpleasant images in the second verse.

Links The idea of something natural, which is at first attractive, having a dark side which gradually turns pleasure into horror, is also explored in 'Death of a Naturalist' and 'Personal Helicon'.

Boost your learning

Read this poem and 'Death of a Naturalist'. Make a Mini Mind Map showing how Heaney is interested in the way natural things can change from light to dark, from attractive to revolting, in both these poems.

Follower

This poem is a detailed memory from the poet's childhood. The first four verses paint a vivid picture of the poet's father ploughing with horses. The poet is present in the picture as a little boy following the plough, sometimes stumbling on the ploughed up ground, sometimes riding on his father's back.

The last two verses bring in new ideas. In the fifth verse the poet tells us that he wanted to grow up and farm like his father and be an expert with the plough (and in fact his family expected that he would do that).

The final verse changes the view we have got of the father and son in the ploughed field. The adult poet realizes that he was often a nuisance following his father about. Then in a climax that sounds more unkind than it actually is (the adult Heaney was to remain very close to his family) he says that now he is grown up and his father is an old man the roles are reversed: it is his father who, as a constant presence in the poet's thoughts, follows him around and 'will not go away'.

Structure This poem is written in six four-line verses. The lines are mostly four beats long, but some are only three. There is no pattern to this. There is a rhyme scheme, ABAB, but some of the rhymes are only half rhymes, and sometimes the lines that should rhyme don't. But the rhymes create a structure which, while not exact, give an order to the poem when it is read aloud. Try it and see.

The structure of the poem is very neat and workmanlike, with its fairly regular rhymes and line lengths. Heaney is trying to show himself to be as skilful in his writing as his father was as a ploughman.

Themes From its simple starting point the poem develops the ideas of what happens to people when they age. The yapping son getting in the way grows up, not to become an expert ploughman like his father, but a poet. The father has grown old and now bothers his son. The poem also paints a very warm and affectionate view of rural life: the father is an expert and does not seem tired or bored by what was actually hard physical work. And it isn't raining or freezing in the remembered scene.

Style and references Heaney uses striking imagery to create a vivid picture of his father's skill at ploughing. Note, too, the simile in line two suggesting the wind blowing out his father's shirt from his shoulders.

the horses strained to his clicking tongue. (line 4) – a simple click was all that he needed to command the well-trained horses.
the sod rolled over without breaking. (line 7) – the furrows were cut neatly and smoothly into the soil.
at the headrig, with a single pluck
of reins, the sweating team turned round. (lines 8–9) – his father could turn the horses round with just one pull of the reins.
The *wing* and the *sock* (lines 5–6) are parts of the plough. The *headrig* (line 8) is the unploughed strip at each end of the field where the horses would turn round to begin the next furrow.

Links 'Digging', 'Death of a Naturalist', 'Cow in Calf', 'At a Potato Digging' and 'Personal Helicon' all contain detailed descriptions from the poet's rural childhood. 'Digging' also compares farming skills – those of his grandfather digging turf for fuel – with the entirely different skills that the poet has acquired.

Boost your learning

? Find all the lines that have exact end rhymes with another line in the same verse.
? Try to find words at the end of lines that half rhyme with other lines in the same verse.
? Find all the descriptions of the skills his father had.
? What picture does the image of his father's *shoulders globed like a full sail strung* conjure up to you?

Mid-Term Break

As a young teenager, the poet waits in the sick bay of the school where he was a boarder (in Derry, the nearest city to the village of Mossbawn where the Heaneys farmed). Arriving home he is surprised to find his father weeping. He is embarrassed by neighbours shaking his hands and saying how sorry they are. His mother is grief-struck, but at this point we don't know what has happened.

Then the ambulance brings the body of his dead brother home. He sits by the bed where the corpse is laid. We learn in the last few lines that he was knocked down and killed by a car and that he was only four years old.

Structure Seven three-line verses with lines of equal length, plus one final line set on its own. The effect of this isolated last line is to focus onto the tragedy of the little boy's death.

Themes The subject and theme of this poem, what it is about and the ideas behind this, are so closely linked that they cannot usefully be separated. The death of a brother was a huge event in Heaney's young life. The poem records his experience of the event quite dispassionately. We see how other people have reacted but learn nothing directly of the inner feelings of the poet. Nor does the poet describe his feelings for his brother up to the time of the tragedy.

This is not callousness, but a device. The poem has such a powerful, tragic effect because it is so emotionally understated. The title suggests a surprise holiday during the school term, but in fact the poet is going home from boarding school to his brother's funeral. The wound on the dead boy's head is simply described as a *poppy*, a rather gentle image. And the power of the last line is that Heaney has saved the most dreadful fact – the boy's age – until the end.

Style and references The language Heaney uses in this poem is plain and straightforward, The only image is the *poppy bruise*, which reminds us of the poppies that are worn on Armistice day in honour of those who died in the two World Wars. The *snowdrops and candles* that *soothed* the bedside of the dead boy convey a sense of someone smoothing a bed or calming a sick child.

Boost your learning

? Why has the poet chosen to begin the poem with the sound of bells *knelling* (ringing)?

? Why has the poet described what the dead boy is lying in as *a four foot box* instead of a coffin?

? There is a sense of shock in the last line of this poem. Find another poem in the selection from *Death of Naturalist* where Heaney uses the last line to deliver a sudden, key idea.

? Re-read 'Digging', 'Follower' and 'Mid-Term Break'.
Make a Mini Mind Map to show all the aspects of
Heaney's relationships with members of his family.

*Look at your finished Mind Map, then take
a break from your revision.*

At a Potato Digging

Although beginning and ending with a scene that the poet is
witnessing, the historical focus of this poem (mainly the third
section) is very important. This is a poem of extended visual
description, and complex ideas about Irish history.

In the first section we see labourers working in a field
harvesting potatoes. A mechanical digger breaks up each
buried row and the men gather the potatoes that it scatters. It
is a bleak scene, one which happens *mindlessly* every autumn.
The men are compared to a line of crows and to fisherman
hauling in a catch. This section concludes with the poet
observing that so much labour is like penance to the earth, as
though the earth which provides them with their food must be
honoured or served by hard work.

The second section is a detailed description of the potatoes
themselves. Potatoes were the staple diet of Irish people for
centuries and the detail the poet goes into reflects the
importance of the crop in the culture he grew up in. But a
strange contrast is developing. The earth is described as *good*,
the *white as cream* potatoes are a *clean birth* but then, when
they are stored in a pit, they become *live skulls, blind eyed.*
This sudden change of mood leads us into the third section.

This describes the horrors of the Irish Potato Famine (1845–8),
when the crop failed for three years in a row, over a million
people starved to death and another million were forced to
emigrate to America. The poet reuses words and images he
introduced in the more upbeat first section, but their effect
now is very different. The line of workers stretched unevenly

across the field is described as *higgledy* in the first section (line 6). The same word is used in the third section to describe people thin as skeletons scouring the land for food during the famine (line 31).This historical section ends with a reference to the present day and the scene that started the poem: the poet imagines that even now when potatoes are being dug you can smell the rot that caused the famine still lingering in the ground.

The last section of the poem returns to the observation of the present-day potato gathering. The gang of men are taking their lunch break. *Dead beat* they rest in a ditch and scatter their crumbs, crusts and slops of tea on to the ground. The poet sees this as them making little offerings to the god of the earth to ensure the famine never comes back. ✪ Find these re-used images and words and explain the effect they have in the first section and how this contrasts with their use in the third section.

Structure First section – four four-line verses, strictly rhyming ABAB. Second section – two loosely structured unequal verses. Third section – six verses each with four short, jaunty lines, rhyming AABB (some of the AA rhymes are half rhymes, all the BB rhymes are full). The effect is to create a cheerful sing-song effect that contrasts grimly with the subject. Fourth section – two four-line verses rhyming, like the first section, ABAB.

Themes The enormous suffering caused by the famine is still a very emotive issue in Ireland. The poet is reflecting on the importance it has in his culture by writing such a long poem which has the fear and horror of famine as its theme. The image of the men *spilling libations of cold tea* suggests that they fear famine might one day come back, that the earth is a food-providing god that has to be honoured. (This is a poetic and emotional idea from Heaney's imagination rather than one which the men would actually hold.)

Unlike many of the subjects Heaney wrote about in his early poems, this is a 'public' poem. The famine was a national tragedy. Heaney is writing about his nation, not his family.

Style and references

higgledy (line 6) – not straight (colloquial).
creel (line 8) – a large wicker basket.
forty-five (line 32) – the Irish Potato Famine began in 1845.
libations (line 53) – an offering to a god or deity.

Links Working with the land and what grows in it is a key idea to the young Heaney growing up in a farming community. 'Digging' also deals in detail with this type of labour, but in a personal rather than a public way.

Boost your learning

?   The poet describes potatoes in several different ways. Find these descriptions.

?   What image of the potato field is conveyed by the words *fish* and *surf*? Picture the field in your mind's eye.

?   Write a sentence or two explaining why the poet talks about the potato diggers breaking a *timeless fast* when they stop for lunch.

Cow in Calf

A simple description of life on the farm where Heaney grew up. He is urging a heavily pregnant cow out of the cow shed. He comments on her enormous size. He is not unkind in hitting her, but she has to move as her time to give birth is close. The description ends with the observation that her heats, the times when she can be made pregnant, and the times when her calves keep coming and going, are part of a pattern as regular as the seasons or the growing and harvesting of crops. Heaney emphasizes the cyclical, natural routine of farm life. But there is a darker side to the end of this poem: the calves 'go' because they are sold, usually for slaughter.

Structure. This poem is loosely structured. The verses each have a different number of lines and the lines are of different lengths, with no pattern to this. There is however one key rhyme. ❂ See if you can find it. Why has the poet used it where he has in the poem? (Answer on p. 73.)

Themes Heaney's view of the cow is practical, as befits a farmer's son, but in mentioning the way the calves go he is perhaps showing that he is not as indifferent to the life and death of animals as a farmer should be. He does not reveal his feelings, but the last line invites us to think about the grim reality of the 'life on the farm'.

Style and references The style of this poem is very simple and direct, as befits the 'everyday' subject of life on the farm.

byre (line 4) – a cattle shed.
my hand/tingled as if strapped. (lines 5–6) – a common punishment in schools in Northern Ireland when Heaney was a pupil was to hit the open hand with a leather strap. This was known as 'strapping'.

Links 'Digging', 'Follower' and 'At a Potato Gathering' all deal in detail with rural life and farm activities.

Personal Helicon

The poet remembers how as a child he was fascinated by wells. No one could stop him from peering down into them. He describes three in particular: one in a brickyard so deep he could not see his reflection, one in a ditch where he had to pull weeds aside to see down, and one where a rat dived out of the undergrowth into the well. He concludes these recollections by saying that adults can't throw things down wells and call out to make echoes. Instead he will, as a poet, rhyme and make echoes that way.

Structure One of the most tightly structured poems from Heaney's first book, *Death of a Naturalist*. Five verses each of four lines of equal length (four beats per line). The verses all rhyme ABAB. Rhymes are important in a poem that has echoes as a key part of its subject matter. ✪ Try to spot the rhyme scheme in every verse.

Themes The descriptions of wells and his fascination with them are a metaphor for his adult role as a poet. He is fascinated and drawn to the idea of writing poems, just as he was drawn to wells as a young boy. The echoes he made by calling down them were a way of expressing himself, as are the poems he is now writing.

And the rat that scared him reminds him that writing poetry is not without its dangers and dark side, the poet may have to confront frightening things about the world and about himself.

This is the last poem in Heaney's first book *Death of a Naturalist*. It is a good poem to end with because it offers a confident statement of what the poet intends to do.

Style and references 'Helicon' was a mountain which, according to Greek mythology, was the home of the nine muses who inspired artists. Anyone who drank the water from the streams that ran off the mountain would be given the gift of being able to write poetry.

windlass (line 2) – a small windmill, usually mounted on a tower of metal rods, used to pump water from a well beneath it.
brickfield (line 5) – a place where clay was dug and fired in kilns to make bricks.
fructified (line 10) – to produce fruit, in this case the weedy growths and blooms on stagnant water.
Narcissus (line 18) – a figure from Greek mythology who fell in love with his own image when he saw it in a pool.

✪ Why has the poet used the colloquial word *scaresome* (think about how it sounds).

Links 'Death of a Naturalist' and 'Blackberry-Picking' both deal with childhood memories that have a dark side. 'Changes' and the second section of 'Wheels within Wheels' also feature water as a key subject.

Boost your learning

'Digging' is the first poem in *Death of a Naturalist*. Make a Mini Mind Map showing how 'Digging' and 'Personal Helicon' connect the two ends of the book.

The Forge

The poet can only see darkness beyond the door into a blacksmith's forge, but he describes what he imagines is happening inside. He can picture what the blacksmith is doing by the noises and a glimpse of sparks. He imagines the anvil to be in the middle of the workshop, it is the most important thing in the forge. He describes it as the altar where the blacksmith devotes himself to his art.

The blacksmith appears at the door. He watches the cars rushing past on the busy road. The poet imagines him remembering a time when there were only horses and horse-drawn vehicles. Impatient with what he now sees outside, the blacksmith turns back to the darkness of the forge to continue working with metal that is *durable*, that will last longer than what he has seen outside. ✪ It is not actually true that the art of blacksmithing will outlast the motor car, so why does Heaney imagine the blacksmith thinking that? (Answer on p. 73.)

Structure This poem is written in sonnet form, which is a strict traditional structure of 14 lines, each line having 10 syllables. Read a few lines out loud and count the syllables with your fingers. (Heaney does vary between 9 and 12 syllables but the basic rule is 10.) Not all the lines rhyme, which is unusual for a sonnet. The rhyme scheme is ABBACDDC, (no rhyme) E (no rhyme) E (no rhyme) E.

A poem about craftsmanship has to be well crafted and Heaney has chosen the strict sonnet form to show his own skill as a poet. ✪ Check the poem to see if this rhyme scheme works out. Read it aloud.

There are different ways to lay out a sonnet but the most usual is to have two verses, of eight lines then six lines. There should be a definite change of mood between the two verses. Heaney has used this form but not put in the verse gap. ✪ Find where the gap between the two verses would come. Does the mood or subject change exactly at this point?

Themes Obviously the poet is speaking fondly of a rural craft. History is dealt with in so far as he is comparing the craft of the past with the traffic of the present.

Heaney has written several poems about the nature of art and what it means to struggle to create works of art, including poems. 'The Forge' is an important example of this theme, so important that the collection in which it was published has part of the first line of the poem as its title. The poet is using the blacksmith as an example of a highly skilled craftsman who 'sticks to his tools' and continues working even though most of the modern world beyond the door to his forge doesn't seem to need what he produces (note the second line describing abandoned ironwork rusting beside the door). The artist can often feel like the blacksmith. The anvil that Heaney imagines in the centre of the working space is compared to a unicorn, a fabulous mythical beast, and to an altar. The blacksmith works at this altar like a priest. He will carry on with what he believes to be lasting and important, in the same way artists and poets works at their craft. All of them must have an almost priestly faith in what they do.

❂ If the poet is using the blacksmith as an example of the almost sacred nature of practising an art, why didn't he make the poem about an artist instead?

Style and references

iron hoops (line 2) – blacksmiths made the iron rims of wagon wheels.
jamb (line 11) – the wooden edge of the door.
bellows (line 14) – used to pump air into a fire to get it red hot.

Links Heaney values work and skills that continue through time and generations. He touches on this in 'Follower' (his father's skill at ploughing with horses) and 'Digging' (his father's and grandfather's skill with a spade). The theme of being an artist is touched on at the end of 'Personal Helicon'.

Boost your learning

?   Heaney uses descriptive details of the forge that appeal to the senses of sight and hearing. Find two examples of each.

?   Why is the anvil described as immovable? (Don't just think about practical reasons!) Relate it to the theme of the nature of art and the work of artists.

Requiem for the Croppies

This poem is 'spoken' by a peasant who fought in the 1798 Irish uprising and died, along with 20,000 other poorly armed and ragged Catholic rebels, at the battle of Vinegar Hill, where they were massacred by a far better equipped Protestant force.

Heaney wrote it to mark the 50th anniversary of another heroic but failed Irish rebellion, the 1916 Dublin uprising. It is a strongly nationalistic poem.

The speaker of the poem tells us that they were a fast-moving, ill-equipped force. They kept barley in their pockets for food as they had no time to make a camp and prepare meals. They improvised ways of fighting to make up for lack of weapons and training, stampeding cattle into the enemy, then running back on foot through hedges where the Protestant cavalry soldiers would get thrown from their horses. The tone up to the point where this is mentioned (line 8) is quite upbeat, the ragged army of farmhands turned rebels is fighting hard and things do not sound too bad. They might be winning. Then the word *retreat* is used, the first hint of defeat (see 'Structure' below for the importance of this word being used where it is).

The last five lines of the poem change to focus towards the horror of the rebels' final battle. They had no cannons, only scythes and pikes, and were massacred. Their bodies were thrown without ceremony into mass graves. The barley they had in their pockets took root and grew and produced a crop on the field above them.

Structure This poem is written in sonnet form, which is a strict traditional structure of 14 lines, each line having 10 syllables. (Read a few lines out loud and count the syllables with your fingers. Heaney does vary the lines between 9 and 12 syllables.) The rhyme scheme is: ABABCDCDEFEFEF.
✪ Read the poem aloud. See if you can hear this pattern of rhymes. Note that Heaney uses one set of half rhymes. Can you tell which lines these are used in?

There are different ways to lay out these lines but the most usual is to have two verses of eight then six lines. There should be a definite change of mood between the two verses. Heaney has used this form but not put in the verse gap. ✪ Find where the gap between the two verses would come. In a brief note explain how the mood of the poem changes.

Themes The theme here is easy to grasp because it is so closely linked to the story that is told of the heroism of the doomed rebels. The speed and energy of their 'war on the run' is compared with the endless cycle of nature.

Style and references The tone of the poem is quick and direct, as if one of the 'Croppies' had just paused on the march to explain what was happening. Then, as it reaches a climax, the pace of the poem is slowed down by one much more lyrical image in line 12 when the scene after the slaughter is described: *The hillside blushed, soaked in our broken wave.*
✪ Explain the poet's use of the word *blushed* in this image.

Croppies – the rebel *croppy boys* were so-called because they cropped their hair short in a period when many men had long hair.

Links The place of death in the unchanging cycle of nature is emphasized in this poem by the crop growing from the barley in the dead men's pockets. 'At a Potato Digging' also looks at dreadful human events and sets them against the endless rhythms of nature and growth.

Boost your learning

?   Think about the anniversary that Heaney wanted to celebrate when he wrote the poem and the barley growing out of the ground on Vinegar Hill in the natural cycle of growth. What might Heaney be suggesting about Irish history?

?   Heaney explores the idea of history and continuity in this poem and in 'At a Potato Digging'. Make a Mini Mind Map showing how the poet explores these linked ideas. Think about time, change and the cyclical nature of the natural world.

'All things that go around come around.'
So do coffee breaks, take one now.

Bogland

The poem begins by comparing the open spaces of the American prairies with the bogs of Ireland. Both are unfenced landscapes. The poet imagines that people living on the prairies look outwards to the distant horizon, but the bogs seem to bring the horizon in, making Irish people look to things nearer to hand, such as the *tarn* (small lake) in verse one.

The soft ground sometimes *crusts* (line 7) but is generally *soft as butter* (line 16). The poet describes things that have been dug up from the bog. He says that coal will never be dug here, but he refers to the turfcutters (the *pioneers* in line 23) who keep digging into the bog for turf which is dried and used as fuel. The poem ends with two myths or folk legends: that the water is seeping into the bog from the Atlantic and that the bog is bottomless.

Structure 'Bogland' is written in seven four-line verses with no end rhyme. The lines are of roughly equal length throughout.

Themes This poem uses the subject of the bogland as a metaphor for Irish history. It is a shared history. Note how the poet uses *we* (line 1) and *our* (line 6). Much of the centre of Ireland is bogland and it is an important symbol of heritage to Irish people. The bogs literally preserve elements of the Irish past that lie buried in it. The poet believes that the land is *kind* (line 16) because it keeps the past locked in it and allows us to dig down and find things that will enrich the future by making people aware of their heritage. Both real things from the past (the skeleton of the now extinct Irish Elk and the butter that people used to bury in the bog to keep it fresh) and folk myths (see above) are mentioned as examples of the Irish heritage that the bogs contain.

So much of Irish history has been about emigration from the famine and domination by England that the eternal unchanging nature of the bogs becomes a potent symbol for Irish identity and sense of homeland.

Style and references The image of the prairies *slicing* the setting sun (line 1–2) as it sinks below the horizon is a powerful visual image to start the poem. It a contrasts the American prairies and the bogs where the *pioneers* dig down into the ground *striking* (line 23) through the bog.

cyclops (line 5) – a one-eyed creature in Greek mythology. – *myth*
tarn (line 6) – a small lake.
Great Irish Elk (line 10) – a large stag-like creature, now extinct. – *History*

❂ Why do you think the skeleton is described as *astounding* and being like a *crate full of air*?

Links The way the poet uses a descriptive subject as an extended metaphor for a much wider theme in this poem can be compared to 'Door Into the Dark'.

Boost your learning

? Why does the poet refer to the men who dig turf out of the bog as *pioneers*? What does the word suggest about Heaney's feelings towards them?

? Why does the poet describe the layers of ground they cut down into as *camped on before*?

Dedicatory poem from Wintering Out

Early on a misty morning the poet is driving past the newly built Long Kesh prison camp in Northern Ireland. The British government has recently introduced internment so that they could imprison without trial people whom they suspected of involvement with terrorist groups. They were sent to Long Kesh, more popularly known as 'the Maze'.

There is a crater by the road caused by a recent terrorist bomb. The scene reminds Heaney of prisoner-of-war films. The wire security fences and machine gun towers of the prison are compared to a German 'Stalag' or prison camp.

The poet then remembers a piece of cynical graffiti he recently saw in a nearby town. *'Is there life before death?'* is a grim joke reversing the old saying 'Is there life after death?' and a sad comment on the restrictions political violence was placing on life in Northern Ireland. The poem ends with Heaney expressing a great sadness, not just for the present 'Troubles' but for the cyclical nature of violence and repression, and the endless battle between Britain and Irish nationhood, that has gone on for centuries.

Structure Four four-line verses rhyming ABAB throughout with lines composed in strict rhythm. Heaney wants this poem to speak directly and powerfully and has chosen a structure which is clear and plain with a strong rhythm.

Themes By choosing this poem as the dedication for his third book *Wintering Out* Heaney is emphasizing the importance of political themes in the poetry he was writing at this time (1972). Internment was a hugely contentious issue, seen by the government as a drastic but necessary measure in its fight against terrorism, but by others as a terrible infringement of human rights. It was central to the 'Troubles' all through the 1970s and Heaney is choosing a 'burning issue' to start his new book of poetry.

But Heaney is not 'waving the flag' for one side over another. Rather he is saddened by the fact that the prison camp is the manifestation of yet another round of oppression and conflict in Ireland's history. It is sadness for the human condition, not a political point, that brings the poem to a climax.

Style and references

Michael Longely (to whom the poem is dedicated) – Northern Irish poet and friend of Seamus Heaney's.
déjà vu (line 8) – the sense that you have seen or experienced something before.

Links 'Casualty', 'The Tollund Man' and 'Punishment' all have strong political comments as part of their themes. 'At a Potato Digging' and 'Requiem for the Croppies' also deal with the cyclical nature of suffering and struggle in Irish history.

The Tollund Man

In the first section the poet has seen a photograph of the black and shrunken, rather eerily preserved figure of the Tollund Man. He was found in a bog in Denmark and is now in a case in a museum in the town of Aarhus in Jutland, Northern Denmark. The man lived in the Iron Age but was so well preserved by the peat bog that the seeds that were in the last meal he ate are still in his stomach. He is wearing only a pointed cap and ropes around his neck and waist. The ropes were probably used to hold him down while he was killed. The poet is fascinated and imagines making the long journey to see the body. He thinks of the Tollund Man as a sort of saint that the goddess of fertility preserved for centuries in the bog.

In the second part of the poem the poet moves on to consider the bog as an almost holy place – an idea which, to someone like Heaney born and raised as a Catholic suggests blasphemy. He remembers the much less peaceful looking corpses of four brothers murdered in the 'Troubles' in Northern Ireland. They had been trailed along railway lines by gunmen, shot and buried in farmyards. The poet wonders that if he prayed to the Tollund Man, who as a pagan priest knew he would one day be killed as a sacrifice, some good may come to Northern Ireland where so many people are being murdered. He muses that maybe the Tollund Man has the power to 'germinate' the dead brothers, to bring them back to life.

The third section of the poem returns to the poet imagining the journey he will make across the flat boglands of Jutland to the museum where the Tollund Man lies. He thinks he will feel some of the sense of regret and ritual that the Tollund Man may have felt as he rode along in a cart towards his death. People will point at the poet passing as they did the Tollund Man, but he will be separated from them by his ignorance of their language. He imagines the *man-killing parishes* of Jutland to be similar to the dangerous rural districts of Northern Ireland. He will feel lost and unhappy, but also at home because he is used to living with death stalking his own country.

Structure Three numbered sections. The first is of five verses, the second and third of three verses each. All verses are four lines long, with short unrhymed lines.

Themes This is in many ways the most difficult of the three poems about bog people covered here. 'The Tollund Man' fascinates Heaney but he does not dwell on the strange appearance of the figure. He is more concerned with imagining the ritual killing of the Tollund Man, who was probably a priest sacrificed to the goddess of fertility. Heaney is also making connections between the ritual death the man suffered and the killings that were then happening in Northern Ireland.

From the appearance of the corpse, the death of the Tollund Man seems to have been much more peaceful than that of the murdered Irish brothers. The Tollund Man knew when he became a priest that he would one day be sacrificed. Heaney is from a Catholic background but feels a connection with the pagan Tollund Man. Heaney imagines visiting the museum in Aarhus and standing a long time in front of the case where the Tollund Man lies. He sees him as representing a ritual order that is missing from the violence-ridden society of Northern Ireland. There is a reverence in the way Heaney describes the Tollund Man. There is a sense of prayer in the list of towns the poet imagines passing through when he makes his journey, his pilgrimage, to the body.

Style and references The opening description of the Tollund man uses vegetable images to compare him to the soil from which he was dug. His head is *peat-brown*, his eyelids are *mild pods*.

girdle (line 10) – the rope round the Tollund Man's waist.
torc (line 13) – an ornamental metal ring worn around the neck by ancient Celts.
fen (line 14) – a watery bog.
stockinged (line 27) – with socks but no shoes.
tumbril (line 34) – a simple cart.

Links 'The Grauballe Man' and 'Punishment' also deal with the Danish and Irish 'bog people'.

Boost your learning

Start a Mini Mind Map by mapping the connections Heaney is making between past and present in this poem. Keep the Mind Map to add to later on.

Before we head 'North' for another collection of poems, take a break.

Funeral Rites

In the first section of this poem Heaney paints a vivid picture of the rituals that went with family funerals. It is a composite drawn from several funerals of relatives he remembers, but the ritual is unchanged. He remembers the events almost affectionately. He certainly approves of the show of grief and respect that was followed by the families who would display the dead person at home with the lid removed from the coffin before the funeral itself.

He recalls how the dead looked in their coffins, especially their hands. He remembers the candle-wax dripping down in the slight draughts made by women as they moved quietly about the room. In one corner stood the coffin lid with its ornamental nails ready to be hammered into place.

The second section moves from these 'peaceful' funerals (we imagine these people to have died from natural causes from the way Heaney speaks) to the need for a ritual suitable for all those who are being killed in the 'Troubles'. He wishes for a ritual that could reconcile the divided community of Northern Ireland. He suggests re-opening the pre-historic burial site at Boyne in the middle of Ireland where the dead from both sides of the 'Troubles' could be laid together. He imagines all the funerals setting out like a great snake of hearses and mourners' cars.

After this great funeral the mourners would drive back to the disputed North and remember their dead lying together. They would not plot revenge. The site at Boyne is pre-Christian and this prompts the poet to remember Ireland's ancient past in the closing section of the third part of this poem. He uses the death of Gunnar, a hero from a Norse myth, as an example for the present. Under Norse law, Gunnar's death should have been avenged, but it was not. Yet Gunnar came back to life in his burial chamber and looked out happily at the moon and sang about honour.

Structure Three sections, all written in verses of four short unrhymed lines. The sections have eight, six and five verses respectively.

Themes Observing the rituals of death and funerals was an important element in the Catholic society in which Heaney grew up and he wishes that such respect for the dead could be given to those dying violently in the 'Troubles'.

As in 'The Tollund Man' and 'Punishment', Heaney draws a comparison between ancient (or in this case mythical) events and the violence in Northern Ireland. He believes that the past has lessons which could help us live together more peacefully in the present. The choice of Gunnar as an example is important. In the Norse Njal's saga it was the fact that Gunnar's death went unavenged that broke a long cycle of feuding and vengeance.

There are some complex references which enhance the ideas Heaney is developing in this poem (although the poem still works if you don't 'get' them). The ancient grave which Heaney suggests as a resting place for all those, Catholic Nationalists and Protestant Loyalists (see 'A Quick Lesson in Irish History' p. 2) killed in the 'Troubles' is close to the River Boyne and the site of the battle in 1690 the anniversary celebrations of which still cause violence in Northern Ireland.

Comparing the funeral processions to a giant snake or serpent also has hidden meanings. St Patrick, who introduced Christianity to Ireland, is supposed to have banished all the snakes from the country (and there are no snakes in Ireland!) thus symbolically purging the country of paganism. Heaney suggests reversing the process as a way to stop the killings in a war where the two sides are separated by their different versions of Christianity.

Style and references The first section of the poem uses a number of striking visual images to paint a picture of the dead in their open coffins: *their dough-white hands/shackled in rosary beads* (line 7-8); *The dulse brown shroud* (line 13); and a vivid description of the faces as *Dear soapstone masks* (line 26).

dulse (line 13) – a type of edible seaweed.
the great chambers of Boyne (line 39) dating from 3200 BC these mounds are believed to cover great burial chambers.
cupmarked stones (line 41) a feature of the Boyne site are stones with little cup-like indentations carved in them.
past Strang and Carling fjords (line 64) – modern day Strangford and Carlingford in Ireland were first settled by Vikings. By noting the Norse origins of these places the poet is able to shift the focus of the final section of the poem to the Norse myth of Gunnar.

Links 'Punishment' and the 'Tollund Man' both compare deaths from history with deaths in the 'Troubles' in Northern Ireland. 'Mid-Term Break' and 'Casualty' deal with the poet's experience of the rituals of death in Northern Ireland.

Boost your learning

Compare the detailed descriptions of the funerals of Heaney's relatives in this poem to that of his brother in 'Mid-Term Break'. Can you identify a difference in Heaney's level of involvement in the funerals and the mourning described in each poem?

The Grauballe Man

Heaney has written a number of poems about the 'bog people', the preserved bodies that have been dug up in peat bogs in Ireland and Denmark. Three – this one, 'The Tollund Man' and 'Punishment' – are discussed in these commentaries. 'The Grauballe Man' is the simplest of the three because it is primarily a description of the body which is now on display in Denmark.

The body has been shrunk and blackened by the peat bog. The poet thinks it looks as if it has been *poured in tar*. He describes its appearance in great detail using a number of striking similes and metaphors (see Style and references below). Water is a constant linking element in his descriptions: different parts of the body are described as a *swan's foot*, a *wet swamp root, a mussel*, an *eel*. ✪ Why should the body remind Heaney of water so strongly? ✪ Explain the possible meanings of the word *cured* in line 22.

At the end of the poem Heaney tells us that the man's throat has been cut. We do not know who did this, or why. The poem ends simply with a description of the wound as opening to a *dark elderberry place*. The wound is dark because of the way the body as been preserved. It is probable that the man ate berries when he was alive. Elderberries are used to make a sweet wine. It is a warm and very human image to end a poem in which the body has been described throughout in cold, watery and dead images.

Structure Six four-line verses without rhymes. The lines are short, two or three beats each.

History

Themes The poet is fascinated by what remains of the bog people after their death. They seem to offer him a window into a long-vanished life. But this poem stays with the idea of describing the strange appearance of the Grauballe Man. It does not seek to make some further idea from the poet's experience of seeing the body. Heaney does not mention why the man died. (One theory about the male bodies found in the Danish bogs, including the Grauballe and Tollund men, is that they were victims sacrificed to the goddess of fertility.)

Style and references This poem uses a lot of similes (*The grain of his wrists/is like bog oak*) and metaphors (*the chin is a visor*) to paint a very detailed picture in words of the appearance of the Grauballe Man. ❂ Find as many examples of similes and metaphors as you can in the poem. Say what effect each one creates.

bog oak (line 7) – a dark, dense often twisted wood.
basalt (line 9) – a black rock.
mussel (line 14) – a shellfish
the Dying Gaul (line 43) – a famous classical statue of a Celtic warrior.

❂ Explain the double meaning use of *mussel* in line 14 to describe the shrunken flesh over the Grauballe Man's hip bones.

Links 'The Tollund Man' and 'Punishment' both deal with preserved bodies dug up from peat bogs.

Boost your learning

From the description of the body that Heaney gives in this poem, visualize what you think it looks like. Draw a Mini Mind Map containing five to ten words or images that you would use to describe it. (These words may help you give your own picture of the Grauballe Man in an exam answer.)

Punishment

Another poem about the 'bog people', bodies that have been dug up from peat bogs in Northern Europe. This time the body is that of a young girl. Heaney presumes that she has been ritually killed for committing adultery. At the beginning of the poem he identifies with her. When she was dug up there was a rope around her neck and he can feel it tugging her towards her death (verse one). He imagines the cold that makes her naked nipples hard and shakes her ribs like the rigging on a sailing boat (verse two). He sees her dead body being weighed down with a stone and sunk into the bog (verse three).

He then describes how she appeared when she was discovered centuries later. He pities her and imagines that before she was killed she was blonde-haired and beautiful. His pity is close to love but then two things happen to the poet's thoughts. First, he admits to an almost sexual thrill at seeing the naked, partly opened body. Then he admits that had he been a member of that tribe which killed her so long ago, he would probably have stayed silent and done nothing to help.

He goes on to consider the ritual punishments that were being handed out to women in Ulster who had befriended British soldiers stationed there. He had seen the victims of these attacks in Belfast. Paramilitary gangs shaved the women's hair, tar was poured over them and they were tied to railings or lampposts. They would have looked not unlike the blackened figure of the girl from the bogs. People would watch but not stop the attacks. Heaney ends the poem by saying that he has done nothing to stop these present day punishments and that he understands and even sympathizes with the tribal need for revenge against women who go against the tribe's 'rules'.

Structure Eleven four-line verses. The lines are all short (no more than three beats) but their lengths are irregular. These short, almost clipped lines give a sense of suppressed anger or violence which suits the subject matter. There is no rhyme scheme, but a lot of half rhymes, for example, *sapling – firkin* (lines 14/16). Say the words aloud to hear the half rhyme.
✪ Read the whole poem aloud very carefully and note the pairs of half rhymes.

Themes This poem covers a lot of complex ideas in relatively few words. What it is about, the subject, and the ideas Heaney wants to explore are inter-twined.

Heaney lays out his own feelings and reactions carefully and without sparing himself. He at first sympathizes with the girl from the bog, and almost falls in love with the person he imagines she was before she died. When comparing that long-ago punishment she suffered to the ones happening in Northern Ireland which he has seen, Heaney connects two punishments handed down by tribes to women for similar 'crimes' that happened centuries apart. ✪ What do you think Heaney's view of time and how man changes down the centuries would be?

Style and references Heaney uses a number of striking similes to describe the girl's body, all of them describing the blackened corpse in terms of natural things. Her nipples are *amber beads*, her shaved head is *a field of stubble*. The short lines of the poem contain a lot of information and ideas and one way Heaney achieves this economy is by using a device called **kenning**. This was used by Old English poets and compresses the two ideas of a simile to make a single image: so the idea that the dead girl's bones were like oak becomes simply *oak-bone*. *Brain-firkin* and *barked sapling* are further examples of kenning. Heaney echoes the sort of poetry that was being written when the girl was alive. The poem also contains examples of alliteration, for example, in the *rigging of her ribs* (lines 7-8) and *her blindfold a soiled bandage* (line 19).

amber (line 6) – petrified sap of trees found in, among other places, Scandinavia (where the girl's body was buried).
barked sapling (line 14) – a young tree that has grown bark.
firkin (line 16) – a fir cone.
cauled (line 39) – a covering for the head, in this case it is the tar that has been poured over the girls' heads.

Links 'The Tollund Man' and the 'Grauballe Man' both deal with the poet's fascination for the preserved bog figures.

Boost your learning

? Use the description section of this commentary and make a flow diagram of the ideas and feelings the poet has at different stages of the poem. Use it to help you with your revision. Start with: 'The poet imagines he is the girl...'

? Read the three poems about people whose bodies have been preserved in bogs: 'The Tollund Man', 'The Grauballe Man' and 'Punishment'. Find the Mind Map you began after reading the commentary on 'The Tollund Man'. Add to it the themes and ideas from the other two poems, especially about the links Heaney sees between past and present.

? Review your Mind Map to make sure you understand the connections and the differences between these poems.

Now take a break to avoid becoming a corpse yourself

Act of Union

In the first section the poet's pregnant wife lies beside him in bed. The baby has made its first movement in her womb. The poet compares this beginning of the process that will lead to birth to flood waters gathering in a bog. He imagines their bodies side by side in bed as two adjacent countries, joined but still separate. He admires her independence, but the first section ends with him being aware of his legacy growing inside his wife. The tone is calm but not especially romantic or tender. It is not a love poem, or a poem about the wonder of childbirth.

The second section changes direction. The poet admits that she will be left with the pain of birth. He imagines the baby growing, becoming an independent force gathering the power to hurt not only its mother, during the birth, but also its father, as it grows and becomes independent. The mood has grown harsh. The poet imagines the infant's fists, his wife's body is *tracked and stretchmarked* and birth is *big pain*.

Structure Each section of this poem is a sonnet. (See the 'Structure' section of the commentary on 'The Forge' for details on sonnets.) In both sections the 14 lines rhyme: ABABCDCDEFEFGG

❍ Check each section of the poem to see if this rhyme scheme works out. Read them aloud.

Themes Both these sonnets are extended metaphors: they use the subject of birth and the image of two people lying in bed together as symbols for the political relationship between Britain and Ireland. The title refers to the Act of Parliament that 'united' Britain and Ireland by abolishing the Irish government in 1800.

The metaphor has many references throughout the poem, including a complex visual one. Imagine a map of Great Britain and Ireland. The poet's wife is Ireland, he is Great Britain. She is lying beside him with her back turned to him, this is the eastern shore of Ireland and he is the bigger land mass over her shoulder.

Heaney says that, like Ireland towards Great Britain, his wife seeks neither to cajole nor ignore him. Nor can she be conquered. He is speaking more of Ireland the country than the woman lying beside him. He recognizes that, as in their baby in his wife's womb, his legacy is contained in the culture and future of Ireland.

The political divisions between Ireland and Great Britain continue the metaphor throughout the second sonnet. Heaney says that he/Great Britain will in the end leave her/Ireland with the pain of the birth/search for freedom. The unborn infant is compared to some sort of hidden growing force of resistance to rule. Already beating at the limits of its world, it will be soon be ready to take on the poet. Its heart beats 'like a war drum'.

The poet's wife has been pregnant before and has suffered the pain of birth before. The images are far from tender. Heaney foresees what she will once again have to go through, just as Northern Ireland regularly goes through violent and painful times. The pain of childbirth and the political struggles and wars in Northern Ireland seem inevitable and unending.

Style and references

province (line 8) – a region within a conquered territory. Northern Ireland is officially referred to as a province.
fifth column (line 19) – a rebel group in an occupied country.
unilateral (line 20) – one sided, especially used in political discussions.

❂ Find all the images of conflict and war in the poem.

Boost your learning

Heaney could have just written a poem about the political connections between Northern Ireland and Great Britain. Why has he chosen to use his wife and the baby growing inside her as an extended metaphor to put forward his ideas instead?

Singing School 2: A Constable Calls

A deceptively simple poem about a memory from childhood. The poet recalls in minute detail a policeman visiting the family farm to record the crops that were being grown. But the poet hardly mentions the policeman, it is his official equipment that fascinates and frightens him.

He describes the policeman's bicycle propped in the sun outside, his hat up-turned on the table, the revolver holster (the police in Northern Ireland have always been armed), and baton case at the policeman's belt.

His father does not report a small patch of turnips he is growing. The poet imagines the *black hole*, the cell in the

59

police station where he fears he father may be put. But the policeman goes away without any trouble.

Structure Nine four-line verses, without rhymes. The lines either have three or four beats, so are of unequal lengths.

Themes This is both a description of a simple family event, and a significant political poem. Nothing much actually happens during the visit. On one level it is the simplest and least threatening of scenes, a policeman on an big upright bicycle collecting trivial details of crops from the farm. But the scene is remembered as being full of menace. This comes from the perspective of the adult Heaney, a nationalist sympathizer naturally wary of the largely loyalist police. Heaney's family were Catholics, the visiting policeman was almost certainly a Protestant. There were many cases of the police attacking Catholics.

The poem was first published in 1975, in Heaney's collection *North*. The 'Troubles' were at their height, and *North* was the book in which Heaney wrote most directly about the conflict in Northern Ireland, and expressed his sympathies for the nationalists who sought political change. Many of his nationalist friends would have spent time in the *black hole* cell in the police station.

The title of the sequence of poems of which 'A Constable Calls' is part, is taken from a line in the famous poem 'Sailing to Byzantium' by another earlier Irish poet, W.B. Yeats. Heaney's sequence as a whole deals with the attitudes and influences that have inspired his own poetry.

Style and references Heaney's choice of images and use of language in this poem creates a sense of terror and violence from a simple everyday scene.

The bicycle dynamo is *cocked back* (line 6), as a gun is cocked ready to fire.
The pedal treads hanging/relieved of the boot of the law (lines 7/8) – echoes with the phrase often used to describe the might of authority, 'the heel of the oppressor'.
the doomsday book (line 30) – the ledger the policeman carries for recording harvests, is described like this because the poet feels it had the power to seal his father's fate.

and the bicycle ticked, ticked, ticked (line 36) – bombs on timers were almost a part of daily life in Northern Ireland at the time this poem was written. The image suggests the violence the boy imagines the policeman could unleash is like a bomb waiting to go off.

Links The other directly political poem that is looked at in these notes is 'Casualty'.

Casualty

The subject of this poem is a man called Louis O'Neill, who frequented a pub in Northern Ireland owned by Heaney's father-in-law.

In the first section the poet paints an affectionate portrait of a simple countryman, a skilled fisherman and nightly heavy drinker. He was so well known he would order drinks just by pointing and miming opening a bottle. He was, in Heaney's eyes, typical of the ordinary working men of the area, but he was forced to live on the dole. There was a high level of unemployment there, especially for Catholics like O'Neill.

The poet describes their casual relationship. O'Neill does not understand the life Heaney leads nor what it means to be a successful writer, and when they meet in the pub Heaney always steers the conversation around to local country matters. But Heaney suggest that O'Neill knew he did this. Heaney thinks O'Neill was much cleverer, more astute than he appeared.

O'Neill liked drinking in pubs. He ignored a curfew that the IRA had imposed on people after the British Army killed 13 Civil Rights marchers in Derry on Bloody Sunday in January 1972 (see Style and references section). The poet describes the tension that everyone in Derry felt. ✪ Write a sentence describing how you think Heaney felt towards O'Neill from what we learn in the first section.

The second section describes the mass funeral of those killed in Derry. Heaney was in the crowd and felt as if he was bound up tight with them in shared grief. He then remembers O'Neill again. O'Neill had always gone his own independent way. Heading off to a pub miles away because he liked the crowd there, O'Neill was blown up and killed by an IRA terrorist bomb. He imagines O'Neill's face at the moment the bomb exploded and hears the dead man asking him why it happened. ✪ Why do the coffins appear to *float* from the cathedral door?

In the third section we learn that Heaney missed the man's funeral, but he describes how he thinks it must have gone, altogether quieter than the mass funeral he saw in Derry. The description of the funeral merges into a description of the poet and O'Neill out fishing in O'Neill's boat, a day of calm and tranquillity. This mood is suddenly broken by the last three lines of the poem where Heaney wishes the man he is remembering so fondly could come back to question him again. ✪ What image does Heaney use to blend the description of O'Neill's funeral into a description of him out fishing when he was alive?

Structure A long poem divided into three unequal sections. The first has three verses of 20, 15 and 11 lines each. The second also has three verses, of 13, 10 and 15 lines. The third section has one long verse of 25 lines followed by a short three-line verse. There is a sense of the poet allowing himself room to think through all his memories of the dead man and to recall the funerals for the victims of Bloody Sunday. One thought leads into another as we read this long poem. ✪ Why do you think the poet has chosen to end the poem with this short little verse? What effect does it create?

The poem is written throughout in short lines of two or three beats. There is no pattern to the variety of beats per line. The lines in the first section rhyme ABAB throughout (right up to KLKLMM for the last six lines of the section, though lines 6/8 voice/eyes is hardly even a half rhyme).

✪ Rhyme hunt. Try marking up the rhyme scheme for the first section. It's best to do it with a friend and to read the poem aloud as some of the rhymes are half rhymes and may not be immediately obvious. Then look for rhymes in the second and third verses.

Themes In describing his relationship with a man whom he sometimes met in a bar, and that man's death, Heaney is telling a simple and fairly straightforward story. But the poem is about much more than the life and death of an unnamed 'casualty'. It is about how simple people are destroyed by violent political events.

O'Neill is presented as a plain good man, who would have worked if there had been a job: a *dole-kept breadwinner/a natural for work* (lines 14/15) ❍ What stopped him from having a regular job? Was it that he was a Catholic in a country where the best opportunities always went to Protestants? Heaney was clearly fond not only of the man, but of what he represented. In a time when people were being murdered by the army on the streets of Derry the images Heaney has of the man's fishing and his easy ways in pubs are very affectionate. Even the funeral as he imagines it, is a calm and quiet affair, contrasting with the mass funeral in Derry.

Written about a time when events in Northern Ireland were at their most dreadful and extreme, this poem sets the simple goodness of a plain man against politics, oppression, violence and fanaticism. The poem carefully balances ambiguities. It was 'his own side', the Nationalist terrorists, that ordered the curfew he broke and planted the bomb that killed him: not the British army. Heaney admires the way the man went his own way. And at the end of the poem, he misses him. He regrets that he will never again have the chance to be questioned by a simple but subtle man who died for no political cause, but just because he liked to go out for a drink.

Style and references Heaney uses simple language and plain but carefully worded imagery throughout the poem to echo the plain but thoughtful language of the dead man. Louis O'Neill was a fisherman and images involving water occur throughout the poem. ❍ Make a list of these 'watery' images. Try to picture them in your mind's eye.

slug (line 27) – a swig.
Provisionals (line 35) – a Nationalist terrorist group, the Provisional IRA (Irish Republican Army).
after they shot dead/the thirteen men in Derry. (lines 41/42) This refers to one of the darkest days of the 'Troubles' in Northern Ireland. In January 1972 British soldiers panicked and opened fire on an unarmed protest march of Nationalist Catholics in the Bogside area of Derry. Thirteen people were

killed. It became known as 'Bloody Sunday'. Tension in Northern Ireland shot up, the IRA, the main terrorist group fighting 'for' the Nationalist cause gained much support and became busy carrying out reprisals. One of these, a bomb planted at some target, accidentally killed O'Neill.

PARAS (line 43) – it was a British Army Paratroop regiment that opened fire in Derry.

surplice and soutane (line 49) – garments worn by Catholic priests.

the screw purling, turning (line 99) – the boat's propeller in the water.

revenant (line 109) – an image, a spirit.

Links The other directly political poem discussed in these commentaries is 'Punishment'. 'Funeral Rites' and 'The Tollund Man' also refer to the violence of the 'Troubles'.

Boost your learning

? The poet never calls the 'casualty' by name. Why do you think this might be? Write a line or two giving your ideas. What effect does Heaney create by just using the term 'casualty'?

? Heaney uses poetic form very subtly. Often a poem which has no obvious overall rhyme and structure creates a rhythm by careful but understated use of beats within lines. This is the case in Casualty.

? Skip back to the 'Poetic Form and Structure' section of this guide and read page 14 which tell you how to 'hear' the beats in a line of poetry and how to scan it with slashes and dashes. Then scan these two extracts from Casualty:

He would drink by himself
And raise a weathered thumb
Towards the high shelf
Calling another rum.

I see him as he turned
In that bombed offending place,
Remorse fused with terror
In his still knowable face,
His cornered outfaced stare
Blinding in the flash.

Try doing this with a friend. Each of you should make a scan of the lines and then compare your work.

then take a break

Changes

The poet and a companion, probably one of Heaney's own children, go through long grass to a little-used water pump. In the country silence the poet imagines he can hear other sounds drawn from his memory: of digging from when the well beneath the pump was dug, of masons mixing mortar for the walls that line the well and the sounds of women who came to use the pump when it provided the only water for their houses.

The poet and his young companion lift the iron lid from the pump. A bird has nested under it. The lid is quickly put back, then the child lifts it again. They see a single egg on a nest and the tail feathers of the mother bird sticking out from the spout where she has hidden herself. She has not flown away and deserted the nest.

The poet describes this simple scene and actions in great detail. It is obviously important to him. He tells his young companion to remember the scene when they have grown up and moved far away and are in a completely different environment, a city with none of the history and sense of belonging that this deserted pump has.

Structure Thirteen unrhymed two-line verses. ✪ Look at the punctuation at the end of the second line of each verse. Does the sense 'run over' from one verse into the next or are the verses generally complete in themselves?

  Themes Unlike the other poems dealing with childhood discussed in these commentaries, this is not about Heaney's own youth. The companion who comes with the poet to the well is obviously young because Heaney says that they will *grow away*.

The atmosphere of this poem, the way the poet describes a rural scene with great clarity and fondness, echoes his earliest poems about his own childhood. The tone catches some of the wonder of childhood. Compare this to the bleak view of the future where the child may one day stand *at the very centre of the empty city* (line 26). ✪ What does Heaney mean when he uses this image? What does he mean exactly when he uses the word *retrace* in line 24?

Style and references. This poem is very simply written, as if the poet were speaking to a young child. But it does contain some very striking images (see 'Boost your learning' section below).

citadel (line 16) – a fortress.

✪ Why does the poet describe the pump under its cover as a fortress?

Links Wells and water are the central theme of 'Personal Helicon', and important in the first two sections of 'Wheels Within Wheels'.

Boost your learning

Explain how these images work:

the slithering and grumble
as the mason mixed his mortar (lines 5/6),
and women coming with buckets
like flashes on their ruffled wings. (lines 7/8).

(Answers on p. 73.)

Seeing Things (1)

The poet and several others are passengers in a small open boat ferrying them from the island of Inishbofin, out in the Atlantic off the west coast of Ireland. The poet describes in clear, spare terms everything about the scene as they prepare to depart: the sights, smells and the motion of the boat that dips and sways every time a new person clambers in.

The boat seems very heavily loaded and the passengers are quiet and nervous. Their combined weight is making it sit very low in the water and they fear the waves could start lapping into the boat even though the sea is calm. Heaney is worried when the engine fires and they move out into the deep water.

The water holds the boat and its passengers up but also frightens the poet because it is so deep. As the boat sails on he can see right down through the clear sea to the boat's shadow moving across the seabed. He can see how fragile the vessel is, and he feels a sudden love for the quiet band of strangers gathered in the boat with him, trusting their small, precious lives to the open boat on the water.

Structure Twenty-two lines with no separate verses. The lines are of varying lengths, but mostly have five beats.

Theme The poet paints a vivid 'picture in words' of the little boat, its cargo of passengers and the water over which it sails. He uses this to build to the sudden realization of how much he cares for the safety not only of himself but of the strangers with whom he is gathered in the boat. In a world where the individual is often king, this poem celebrates our common humanity.

Style and references

turfsmoke (line 2) – smoke from the peat fires in cottages.
boatslip (line 2) – a stone ramp into the sea from which boats are launched.
gunwales (line 8) – the top lip of the side of an open boat.
ship (line 9) – take on water.
heft (line 13) – to lift up, usually to judge the weight of something.

Boost your learning

The poet uses some unusual 'condensed' words and phrases in the poem: *shilly-shallied/scaresomely* (lines 4/5) and *seeable-down-into water* (line 18). Why do you think he has chosen such language? Make a Mini Mind Map of your ideas.

Further Reading You can get an interesting view on the theme that Heaney develops in this poem by doing some further reading. Heaney's close friend Derek Walcott, another Nobel prize-winning poet, has written a poem about sharing a bus with a group of strangers on his native island of St Lucia in the West Indies. He develops the same theme in a very different setting. The poem is called 'The Light of the World' and can be found in his collection *The Arkansas Testament*.

Field of Vision

A woman sits and stares out of a window towards the rural landscape beyond. It is an ordinary view of a field and a mountain beyond, very common in Northern Ireland.

We do not know who she is nor where it is that she sits. We do not know why the poet says he remembers her. But we know she sees the trees come into leaf then the leaves falling, so she is watching through the window for years on end. We imagine she is old and resident in an old peoples' home, or a mental health patient in an institution. She never looks at the television next to the window, preferring the view of the world outside.

Heaney does not pity her. Instead as the poem closes he marvels at what she sees. The view she stares at is commonplace, but such a view becomes more strange and focused the longer you stare at it. He compares what she sees to the view that an 'ordinary' (free to move about) person sometimes sees when they stop by the road and look over a farm gate and become drawn into the landscape across the fields.

Unlike many of Heaney's poems which reach definite conclusions, especially the earlier ones in this collection, there is a sense of mystery about both the woman and the view she stares at.

Structure Five four-line verses, with no rhymes. The lines are of four or five beats.

Theme One way of summing up this poem is to remember that one should 'never judge by appearances'. The woman may be living a very limited life by most people's standards, but Heaney praises her for never giving in to emotions or self-pity. He thinks she sees something special in the view, something that can only be discovered by long and disciplined watching.

Style and references This is a plainly written poem. He will not 'give in' to extravagant or complex language, just as the woman in the poem will not give in to self-pity. Both her resolve and the style of the poem exude quiet strength.

A well-braced gate (line 14) – a strong well made gate with diagonal cross-pieces to keep it from sagging.

Boost your learning

? Write a sentence in your own words describing how you think the poet feels about the woman.

? Stare out of the window for a while, like the woman in 'Field of Vision'. Try staring for a full five minutes, then making a quick list of all the details you noticed that would have missed if you had just taken a quick glance. Make a descriptive poem of the view from your window from this list of details.

that's enough staring – take a break and give your eyes a rest

Wheels within Wheels

The last poem in these commentaries loops back to a theme that Heaney explored in many of his earliest published poems: childhood and loss of childhood innocence. In the first section he describes how, as a boy, he loved turning his bicycle upside down and spinning the back wheel by turning the pedals with his hands. He describes watching the spokes disappear into a blur of speed. The air hummed. He threw a potato into the spokes and it was dissolved into a flying mush. He poked a straw into the spokes and it *frittered*. He was amazed at the way the momentum of the spinning wheel took over from your hand turning the pedals. It was a discovery of power for the young boy. The poet compares this to discovering a belief, almost like a life-force in the turning wheel.

The second section describes how he continued this game by taking the bicycle down to a muddy water hole where cattle went to drink. He describes the water and the plume of spray he could make by dipping the upturned rear wheel into the water and spinning the wheel. He did this with great pleasure for weeks until the water rusted and jammed the chain and crank of the bicycle.

The third section describes his disappointment when this happened. Nothing was quite as good as this after the bicycle broke, until one day, long after these events, he went to a circus. There was an act in which artistes dressed as cow girls came out spinning lassoes around themselves. The poem ends with a return to joy. In a series of short phrases and words he sums up the excitement he felt at rediscovering this life-enhancing sense of the beauty of things spinning. The last word in the poem, *stet*, is a term used in publishing. It means literally 'let it stand', and is used where something has been altered but should be left as it originally was. ❂ Why has the poet used this little-known word to end the poem?

Structure. Three unequal unrhymed sections of 17, 20 and six lines. The lines are generally of five beats each.

  Theme The theme of this poem is childhood expectation, disappointment, then rediscovery later on of the original joy. It is the poem of a man old enough to have experienced these three phases. The subject of the bicycle wheel, of the beauty and childhood marvel of spinning things, can be seen as symbolic of many things that are wonderful in youth then lose their wonder as reality and time take over, then are rediscovered in a different form much later on.

Style and references The title is a pun. The bicycle literally has wheels within wheels: the cog wheels at the centre of the back wheel. But the expression is also used to describe 'the hidden processes of life'.

The simple and logical descriptions in the first two sections of the way the poet used the bicycle's spinning wheel to achieve the sense of power and wonder contrast with the shorter, much more compressed and complex way he conveys the wonders of the circus.

preternaturally (line 4) – beyond or surpassing the natural.

momentum (line 14) – the impetus or energy created by a moving object (the wheel).

coterminous (line 17) – two things that meet at their boundary are coterminous. In this complex image that ends the first section of the poem, Heaney is saying that the wheel was important to him because it symbolized the idea that belief had taken up and spun the things he wanted to believe in an orbit (the rim of the wheel) that matched exactly the longing for belief.

turbid (line 25) – thick and muddy.

sump (line 26) – a marshy hollow where water collects.

regenerate clays (line 36) – Heaney uses this phrase with two meanings in mind: to make (the clay thrown up by the spinning wheel) better than before, and, in a religious sense, to be spiritually born again.

nimbus of old glit (line 37) – a nimbus is a bright or shining cloud, 'old glit' is the poet's way of describing old glitter, the faint light that is caught as the muddy water is spun up by the wheel.

lariat (line 41) – a lasso.

perpetuum mobile (line 42) – Latin for 'perpetual motion'.

pirouette – (line 42) – a dance move in which the dancer spins round and round on one foot.

tumblers (line 43) – acrobats.

jongleurs (line 43) – entertainers: jugglers or minstrals.

ring a rosies (line 43) – a game in which children dance in a circle.

stet (line 43) – see explanation on p. 71.

✪ Compare the vocabulary Heaney uses in an earlier poem about water, 'Personal Helicon', with the language he uses in this poem. What are the differences?

Links 'Personal Helicon' also deals with the poet's continuing interest in the theme of water.

Boost your learning

?   Explain the double meaning in the first line of the poem. Why was the discovery of what he could do by spinning the wheels of the up-turned bicycle so important to the young poet?

?   *And showered me in my own regenerate clays* (line 36) – use the commentary you have just read to draw a Mini Mind Map explaining the full meaning of this complex line.

ANSWERS

Page 37, 'Cow in Calf'
Heaney rhymes two short lines, the second from last and last in the poem, using the words *lowing/going*. It creates a sense of the poem being 'rounded off', especially when you read it aloud.

Page 39, 'The Forge'
The blacksmith believes in his skills and his craft despite the logic which says that horses will never come back and replace motor cars. He has faith in what he does, and faith goes beyond reason. Heaney admires this in the blacksmith and believes artists to have the same kind of belief in their work.

Page 65, 'Changes'
the slithering and grumble/as the mason mixed his mortar (lines 5–6). This suggests the noise and the motion of the wet mortar being mixed ready for mason to build the well wall.

and women coming with buckets/like flashes on their ruffles wings (lines 7–8). Imagine the women, probably with shawls wrapped around them, with their arms out holding white buckets. This would look like flashes of white on the outstretched wings of a bird.

TOPICS FOR DISCUSSION AND BRAINSTORMING

One of the best ways to revise is with one or more friends. Even if you're with someone who hardly knows the text you're studying, you'll find that having to explain things to your friend will help you to organize your own thoughts and memorize key points. If you're with someone who has studied the text, you'll find that the things you can't remember are different from the things your friend can't remember – so you'll help each other.

Discussion will also help you to develop interesting new ideas that perhaps neither of you would have had alone. Use a **brainstorming** approach to tackle any of the topics listed below. Allow yourself to share whatever ideas come into your head – however silly they seem. This will get you thinking creatively.

Whether alone or with a friend, use Mind Mapping (see p. vi) to help you brainstorm and organize your ideas. If with a friend, use a large sheet of paper and thick coloured pens.

Any of the topics below could feature in an exam paper, but even if you think you've found one in your actual exam, be sure to answer the precise question given.

TOPICS

1 How the 'bog people' were a source of inspiration for Heaney.
2 Heaney's attitude towards his family and their traditional way of life.
3 Heaney's responses to the political violence of the 'Troubles'.
4 The role of nature in Heaney's poetry.
5 Growing up and loss of innocence in Heaney's poetry.
6 The importance of history to Heaney.

HOW TO GET AN 'A' IN ENGLISH LITERATURE

In all your study, in coursework, and in exams, be aware of the following:

- **Characterization** – the characters and how we know about them (e.g. what they say and do, how the author describes them), their relationships, and how they develop.
- **Plot and structure** – what happens and how it is organized into parts or episodes.
- **Setting and atmosphere** – the changing scene and how it reflects the story (e.g. a rugged landscape and storm reflecting a character's emotional difficulties).
- **Style and language** – the author's choice of words, and literary devices such as imagery, and how these reflect the mood.
- **Viewpoint** – how the story is told (e.g. through an imaginary narrator, or in the third person but through the eyes of one character – 'She was furious – how dare he!').
- **Social and historical context** – influences on the author (see 'Background' in this guide).

Develop your ability to:

- Relate **detail** to **broader content, meaning and style**.
- Show understanding of the author's **intentions, technique and meaning** (brief and appropriate comparisons with other works by the same author will gain marks).
- Give **personal response and interpretation**, backed up by **examples** and short **quotations**.
- **Evaluate** the author's achievement (how far does the author succeed and why?)

If studying a poem, ask yourself:

- What is the emotional **tone**.
- What is the subject and underlying **theme**?
- What is the **structure** and **rhyme scheme** (if any)?
- What effects are made by the **choice of words** and by **imagery**?

Planning

You will probably have about an hour for one essay. It is worth spending about ten minutes planning it. An excellent way to do this is in the three stages below.

1 **Mind Map** your ideas, without worrying about their order yet.
2 **Order** the relevant ideas (the ones that really relate to the question) by numbering them in the order in which you will write the essay.
3 **Gather** your evidence and short quotes.

You could remember this as the **MOG** technique.

Then write the essay, allowing five minutes at the end for checking relevance, and spelling, grammar and punctuation. **Stick to the question**, and always **back up** your points with evidence in the form of examples and short quotations. Note: you can use '. . .' for unimportant words missed out in a quotation.

A note on quotes

You should always use quotes in coursework essays and examination answers to support the things you are saying about the poems. But there is a difference between using quotations to underline your arguments and using them as 'padding' without really explaining why you have chosen them.

Here are few basic rules to remember when using quotes:

◆ Quotations should be used to carry forward the ideas of your essay. Don't use a quote without introducing it by saying why you are using it.
◆ Put inverted commas (' ') around quotes.
◆ Keep the quote short – just use the line or part of the poem that exactly fits in with your essay. Try to keep quotes to a maximum of three lines.
◆ Make sure you quote exactly what the poet wrote!

◆ If the quote you are using is two or more complete lines long, start a new line when the poet does, for example:
'I can feel the tug
of the halter at the nape'
If you are quoting only part of two lines use a slash to show where the line break comes, for example:
'the tug/ of the halter'.

Don't explain in your own words what the poet is saying at a particular point and then quote the line. This wastes time. Unless the meaning is particularly obscure, let the quote speak for itself. So don't write:

The poet describes the big fat frogs sitting on tufts of earth with their necks pumping and pulsing in these lines:
'gross-bellied frogs were cocked/ on sods: their necks pulsed like sails.'

This is just repetition. But you could use this same quote usefully when describing the way the poet uses the images of the frogs:

The poet wants to show the frogs as ugly, unpleasant and somehow dangerous creatures who have taken over the pond which was once a place to play and enjoy:
'gross-bellied frogs were cocked/ on sods: their necks pulsed like sails.'

This shows that you have chosen the quote as evidence to support an idea you have about the poem and how it works.

Short quotes can be neatly inserted into the flow of your sentence. Writing about how the poet describes the berries in 'Blackberry-Picking', you might say:

The poet uses powerful sensual imagery to describe the berries in terms of blood. The first berry picked was *'a glossy purple clot'* with a taste *'like thickened wine*: *summer's blood was in it.'*

Here you have got two quotes to support your idea of the blackberry-blood imagery neatly slotted into one sentence.

Model answer and essay plan

The next (and final) chapter consists of a model answer to an exam question on Seamus Heaney, together with the Mind Map and essay plan used to write it. Don't be put off if you don't think you could write an essay like this yet. You'll develop your skills if you work at them. Even if you're reading this the night before the exam, you can easily memorize the MOG technique in order to do your personal best.

The model answer and essay plan are good examples for you to follow, but don't try to learn them off by heart. It's better to pay close attention to the wording of the question you choose to answer in the exam, and allow Mind Mapping to help you to think creatively.

Before reading the answer, you might like to do a plan of your own, then compare it with the example. The numbered points, with comments at the end, show why it's a good answer.

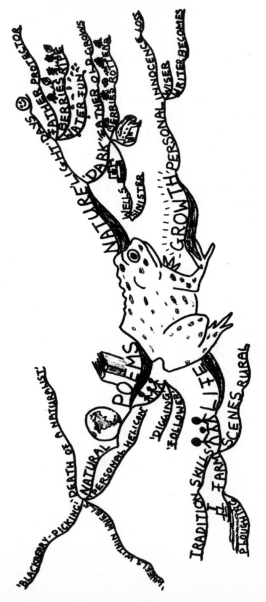

QUESTION

Discuss how Seamus Heaney portrays childhood and the loss of innocence that accompanies growing up.

PLAN

First think about the poems where these ideas are covered. They divide into two thematic groups:

◆ Poems about loss of innocence in terms of nature and childhood experiences. 'Death of a Naturalist', 'Blackberry-Picking', 'Personal Helicon' and 'Wheels within Wheels' are the ones that should by now spring to mind. (Try to talk about this last poem as it comes from the 'other end' of the selected poems from *Death of a Naturalist* and this will show you have read more than the poems in the opening sections of the book!)

◆ Poems about growing up and moving away from the family: 'Digging' and 'Follower' are the two key poems here.

Your plan should contain the following general points (look at the Mind Map to see how these connect):

◆ Love of nature.

◆ Ability to describe nature vividly, often through the eyes of a child.

◆ Sense of security and safety gradually being eroded, by nature 'tricking him.'

◆ Playing and following instincts giving way to more responsible and cautious actions.

◆ Relationship with father – admiration for his skills, and for those of grandfather (ancestors).

◆ Wishing to follow in the farming tradition.

◆ Now wants to write not farm.

◆ Father now stumbles behind as son seeks independence in his craft of writing.

◆ Still respects and loves the farming 'world' but wants to be at a distance from it.

Don't be afraid to make a personal response to a poem, saying how it makes you feel. This shows you are engaged with the writing at an emotional level.

ESSAY

Several of the best known poems from Heaney's first book 'Death of a Naturalist' offer striking descriptions of his childhood on his parents' farm.[1] They deal with a recurring theme: the loss of innocence that growing up inevitably causes.[2]

This is often expressed in terms of changes in the natural world in which the poet played as a child, and his responses to these changes. In 'Blackberry-Picking' he recalls the pleasures of gathering blackberries. Yet by the time the poem reaches its conclusion the berries have rotted. Instead of the rich dark berries whose 'flesh was sweet/ like thickened wine,' now there is a 'fur/ a rat-grey fungus, glutting on our catch'. The young Heaney cries at this betrayal by nature. But the poet steps outside the limits of the child's thinking when he concludes by saying 'Each year I hoped they'd keep, knew they would not.'[3]

The importance of the poem 'Death of a Naturalist' to Heaney is shown by the fact that it is also the title of his first collection. The poem operates in a similar way to 'Blackberry-Picking', a simple childhood scene is remembered in clear, vivid images which suggests magic, security and wonder. But as time passes the darker, more ugly reality of the world is revealed.[4]

This poem has a more definite conclusion than 'Blackberry-Picking', where we feel the child could go out next year and collect the berries again even though he knows what will happen. The naturalist in 'Death of a Naturalist' dies. The boy who goes out to gather frogspawn from the pond is revolted by the frogs that have taken over when he makes a second visit. 'Naturalist' has a double meaning here: a boy interested in nature and a young innocent 'natural' person. By the end of the poem the boy has lost some of his love of nature and also some of his innocence.[5]

The change in the natural world that is described to convey symbolically the change in the boy's thinking is dramatic. The scene to begin with is almost enchanted:

'There were dragonflies, spotted butterflies,
But best of all was the warm thick slobber
of frogspawn ...'

Compare the atmosphere of these lines to the descriptions of the hatched frogs in the second verse of the poem:

'The slap and plop were obscene threats. Some sat
Poised like mud grenades, their blunt heads farting.'

The poem ends with the boy running away, but he cannot run away from the changes that are happening to him and his view of the world as he grows up.

This way of using the natural world to symbolize change is returned to in a much later poem. 'In Wheels within Wheels' he remembers using his upturned bicycle as a sort of water wheel in their farm pond. It was a wonderful game and he was entranced by the way the just-immersed back wheel 'Spun lace and dirt-suds there before my eyes.'

The disappointment that experience brings here is that the water rusts and finally seizes the bike chain. The poet ends the second section of this poem by noting sadly: 'Nothing rose to the occasion after that'.

But this poem has a happier ending than 'Blackberry-Picking' or 'Death of a Naturalist'. Visiting a circus as an adult he sees all manner of spinning things that remind him vividly of the magic the bike wheel once held for him, and the magic is still as strong as ever.[6]

Growing up for Heaney is also about discovering self-determination. He was the eldest son of a farming family. It was assumed he would take on the farm, but in two closely linked poems, 'Follower' and 'Digging', we learn that he wants to become not a farmer but a writer.

In 'Digging' he details in glowing terms the skill with a spade that both his father and grandfather had. *Pride in his ancestry*

'By God, the old man could handle a spade.
Just like his old man.'

'My grandfather cut more turf in a day
Than any other man on Toner's bog.'

The admiration is clear, but in the end Heaney chooses a different tool, a pen. _Which fits as 'snog as a gun'._

In 'Follower' we have another vivid farm scene, his father ploughing a field. Heaney is the young boy who follows after his father. He often stumbles and is sometimes carried on his father's back. The man commanding the plough is a hero in the boy's eyes, big and fast moving as a sailing ship with 'His shoulders globed like a full sail strung/ between the shafts' as his shirt blows out in the wind. The boy at first wants to be like him:

'I wanted to grow up and plough,
To close one eye, stiffen my arm.'

By the end of the poem things have changed. The boy has grown up to be a poet and the roles are now reversed, 'it is my father who keeps stumbling/behind me, and will not go away.' He does not mean that his father literally follows him around, but that his father is often, perhaps too often, in his thoughts.[7]

Thus through recording how nature changes and using this as a symbol for the equally inevitable changes that occur as one grows up, and through poems which detail how Heaney admired but ultimately rejected the life style and traditional skills of his farming background, the poet explores the theme of growing up and losing childhood innocence in a variety of fascinating and moving ways.[8]

WHAT'S SO GOOD ABOUT IT?

1 Shows knowledge of a number of poems.
2 Compares and links poems together.
3 Well-chosen quotes used to support ideas.
4 Explanations of how key poems work.
5 The question is properly considered and responded to.
6 Background knowledge (of the poet and his life) is given.
7 Subject and themes clearly explained.
8 Answer ends with a 'rounding up' referring back to the question.

GLOSSARY OF LITERARY TERMS

alliteration   repetition of a sound at the beginnings of words, e.g. *shilly-shallied*.

context   the social and historical influences on the author.

foreshadowing   an indirect warning of things to come, often through imagery.

image   a word picture used to make an idea come alive; e.g. a **metaphor**, **simile**, or **personification** (see separate entries).

imagery   a word picture used to make an idea come alive.

irony   (1) where the author or a character says the opposite of what they really think, or pretends ignorance of the true facts, usually for the sake of humour or ridicule; (2) where events turn out in what seems a particularly inappropriate way, as if mocking human effort.

kenning   a device which compresses the two ideas of a simile to make a single image; e.g. *oak-bone* in 'Punishment'

metaphor   a description of a thing as if it were something essentially different but also in some way similar e.g. *Wearing a poppy bruise*. An 'extended metaphor' expands an idea, sometimes into a whole poem.

onomatopoeia   a word which echoes the sound it describes.

personification   a description of something (e.g. fate) as if it were a person.

prose   language in which, unlike verse, there is no set number of syllables in a line, and no rhyming.

setting   the place in which the action occurs, usually affecting the atmosphere; e.g. the flax dam in 'Death of a Naturalist'.

simile   a comparison of two things which are different in most ways but similar in one important way; e.g. in 'Casualty', the coffins floating *Like blossoms on slow water*.

structure   how the poem or a narrative is organized.

theme   an idea explored by an author; e.g. death.

viewpoint   how a story is told; e.g. through action; or in a poem, who is 'speaking'

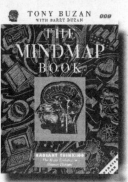